COGNITIVE BEHAVIOURAL THERAPY

The Essential Guide

Cognitive Behavioural Therapy – The Essential Guide is also available in accessible formats for people with any degree of visual impairment. The large print edition and eBook (with accessibility features enabled) are available from Need2Know. Please let us know if there are any special features you require and we will do our best to accommodate your needs.

First published in Great Britain in 2012 by
Need2Know
Remus House
Coltsfoot Drive
Peterborough
PE2 9BF
Telephone 01733 898103
Fax 01733 313524
www.need2knowbooks.co.uk

SB ISBN 978-1-86144-231-4
Cover photograph: Dreamstime

Contents

Introduction

This book is for those who want to learn how to feel better – a user's manual for your mind. Whether you have feelings of depression, anxiety, worry, stress, anger, other challenges, or if you just want to increase your wellbeing, cognitive behavioural therapy (CBT) works. CBT is a way to harness the natural abilities of your brain to your advantage.

CBT is the most proven type of talking therapy. Adults, young people and children can all successfully use CBT. A wealth of research shows CBT is effective for most, if not all, emotional and mental health problems plaguing humanity. And the numbers in Britain do indeed indicate just that – a plague. One in six of us has depression or a chronic anxiety disorder. You are not alone.

CBT is so successful, not because it is some sort of magic wand or panacea, but because it is a set of universally effective tools for managing and changing how we feel, think and act. It is based on research which shows links between our thoughts and our emotions. CBT encompasses a growing number of methods that use these connections and other natural characteristics of our minds and brains.

When you know how a tool works, you can use it more effectively. This book is a tool for understanding how these techniques work in your brain and offers easy to follow, step-by-step methods for identifying the thoughts, feelings and actions that are key to feeling better – and advice on how to change them. It provides clear methods, including charts and exercises for depression, anxiety, obsessive-compulsive problems, worry, stress, and anger. The book and help lists provide further resources for specific problems.

You can use this book to make changes in your own behaviour or to help someone else. Or use it to work along with a therapist (see the section on how to find one).

This book is your tool kit, your essential guide for harnessing your emotional and psychological life. As you become adept at the methods, you are invited to adapt and modify them, and invent your own, for yourself and for those you know, now and in the future. Everything you need to feel better and increase your wellbeing is right here on these pages. You can start right now.

Disclaimer

This book cannot be used to diagnose a specific clinical disorder, nor should it take the place of professional advice. If your emotions, thoughts or actions are interfering with your daily functioning, you may be best served by seeking professional help. Working with a book like this can help, but it may not be enough. Research shows that working with a therapist (as with going to a teacher for any kind of learning) helps people feel better faster, compared to going it alone. If you would like to get some professional help, ask your general practitioner (GP) and they may refer you to a mental health professional either through the National Health Service, or privately if that is an option for you. Organisations listing accredited therapists and other resources are listed in the help list at the end of this book.

Chapter One

What is Cognitive Behavioural Therapy (CBT)?

'The best years of your life are the ones in which you decide your problems are your own. You do not blame them on your mother, the ecology, or the president. You realize that you control your own destiny.'

Dr Albert Ellis

Cognitive behavioural therapy defined

CBT is a method for changing how we feel through changing how we think.

Terms defined

- Cognitive: of, relating to, conscious intellectual activity; thinking, reasoning, remembering, imagining.
- Behaviour: manner of behaving or conducting oneself; the responses made by an organism in any situation.
- Therapy: a course of treatment designed to heal and improve mental and/or physical health and wellbeing.

Thinking changes the brain

Practice *does* make perfect. It turns out that *anything* we do over and over again – including thinking the same thoughts – triggers our brain tissue to strengthen those underlying circuits of brain cells. Our brain tissue can't tell the difference between practising the violin or repeatedly thinking negative thoughts – it just takes its marching orders from the fact that we keep doing the same thing repeatedly, as though we're trying to learn something (see chapter 2 for more details). Research shows that negative thoughts are instrumental in depression, anxiety and other problems. Hence, shifting this negative thinking improves our mood. This process is at the core of CBT.

It can feel as though our thoughts and feelings happen 'to' us, are visited upon us. CBT helps us manage our brain activity to our own advantage, improving how we feel no matter what sort of problems we encounter. Whereas our thoughts and feelings can run away with us at times, CBT offers methods to take the reins of our brains back into our own hands.

'The general finding is that therapy is as effective as drugs in the short term and that both are better than no treatment. In the longer term, therapy has more long-lasting effects than drugs.'

London School of Economics, The Depression Report 2006.

CBT techniques tend to fall into one of three categories (see chapters 5-9 for step-by step instructions):

- Quieting the mind – to retune our brain activity when it gets out of balance.
- Stopping harmful thoughts – feelings and behaviours
- Replacing harmful thoughts – feelings and behaviours

CBT facts

- CBT is an active process.
- The focus is on here-and-now techniques.
- You can learn it through a book, online, in a group, or with a therapist.
- Shorter courses of treatment 8-16 weeks have been shown to be effective, compared to longer courses for other types of therapy.
- CBT is as effective as medication in reducing many symptoms.
- CBT is better than medicine for decreasing recurrence of depression or anxiety.
- CBT is the most evidence-based form of talking therapy.

Origins of CBT

At a time when psychoanalysis of our past was thought to be sufficient for recovery from mental health problems, two researchers in particular were considered 'the fathers of CBT'. Working separately in the 1950s and 60s, they both found a powerful connection between thoughts and feelings. They also found that by changing how we think and behave, we can rid ourselves of depression, anxiety and many other problems.

Dr Albert Ellis (1913-2007) came to these ideas through his personal experience. He had a difficult childhood including neglect, numerous hospitalisations for physical problems and having to leave school early because of the Great Depression of 1929. As a teenager, he forced himself to talk to 100 women he didn't know in a month as a means of curing himself of his overwhelming shyness, and it worked! These experiences inspired him to develop his own pragmatic form of therapy called 'Rational Emotive Behaviour Therapy' (REBT) that focuses on changing thoughts and behaviours, rather than only analysing the past. He found that it was not life's events, per se, that upset us, but our thoughts about them. This is considered the earliest form of CBT. Dr Ellis was famous for being a straight talker and down to earth. See the book and help list for more resources about Dr Ellis' large and esteemed body of work (www.albertellisinstitute.org).

'Many CBT concepts and methods overlap with those of Buddhism, and there has been increasing work about the links between the two.'

Dr Aaron T Beck (born 1921, he goes by 'Tim') came across similar concepts when he was a young doctor conducting research on the causes of depression. Like Dr Ellis, Beck was also trained in the psychoanalytic theories of the day, but his research was finding they weren't true! Instead, Dr Beck found that people with depression had ongoing, spontaneous, frequent negative thoughts. He called these 'automatic thoughts', and found they fell into three categories of negative thoughts: about themselves, their future or the world more generally. Furthermore, Dr Beck found that by using step-wise methods to stop these thoughts, depression lifted and mood greatly improved. This was the start of an auspicious and highly successful career, including worldwide research on the evidence-base of these methods in treating a wide variety of disorders including depression, schizophrenia, bipolar disorder, eating disorders, drug abuse, anxiety disorders, personality disorders and many medical conditions with psychological components (www.beckinstitute.org). See the book and help lists for more information.

Many others have added to the field immeasurably. Three more are mentioned here. Dr Arnold A. Lazarus (born 1932) is credited as the first to expand CBT beyond emotions and thoughts and incorporated all aspects of human functioning including physical sensations, visual experiences, biological factors and relationships. He called his variation of CBT 'behaviour therapy' (*Behaviour Therapy and Beyond*, 1971). He was forward thinking in using CBT in groups and was the first to use it with children.

Dr David M. Clark is an international leader in the field including in the UK, Ireland and the US. He has demonstrated the effectiveness of CBT for anxiety disorders including post-traumatic stress disorder (PTSD) and medical anxiety (formerly called hypochondriasis). He worked with the National Health Service in the UK in making CBT central in their clinical practice guidelines. He is currently the Director of the Centre for Anxiety Disorders and Trauma at the Maudsley Hospital and Professor of Psychology at the Institute of Psychiatry, King's College, London.

'Depression is the leading cause of disability worldwide.'

World Health Organisation

Dr Martin E.P. Seligman (born 1942) did ground-breaking research in the late 1960s leading to the concept 'learned helplessness'. These studies showed how exposure to uncontrollable stress can lead to depression and even increase your vulnerability to cancer (see chapter 8 for more information). More recently, Dr Seligman's work has focused on how to increase happiness (rather than how to reduce mental health problems). These methods are being piloted in 60 schools in the UK as described below (Learning happiness in school)

Who can use CBT?

Depression, anxiety and/or stress are the most common mental health problems the world over.

Everyone can use CBT to improve their lives. Research shows that adults, children, couples and families all benefit from CBT. You can use it if you're struggling with specific mental health symptoms or if you want to improve your sense of wellbeing.

CBT is effective in treating a wide variety of problems, some of which are listed below. CBT is not a panacea but a set of techniques that addresses universal aspects of the human condition and this is why it has been applied successfully, to just about most, if not all, mental health problems.

- Alcohol misuse.
- Anxiety.
- Attention deficit disorders.
- Bipolar disorder.
- Chronic fatigue.
- Chronic pain.
- Depression.
- Drug misuse.
- Eating disorders.
- Medical anxiety (formerly called hypochondriasis).
- Obsessive-compulsive disorder (OCD).
- Panic attacks.
- Phobias.
- Postnatal depression.
- Post-traumatic stress disorder (PTSD).
- Schizophrenia.
- Self-harm.
- Sleep disorders.
- Smoking cessation.
- Stress.
- Trauma recovery.

There is over 50 years of research and literally thousands of scientific articles show the effectiveness of CBT. Numerous studies find that CBT combined with medication is the most effective treatment for depression in both adults and adolescents. Furthermore, CBT protects against recurrences of depression and anxiety problems.

'Almost one in six people in the UK, some six million people, suffer from depression or anxiety disorders or both.'

Psychiatric Morbidity Study, UK Govt 2002.

Getting started – your thought survey

This survey provides the groundwork for core CBT techniques including those in the chapters ahead. How to complete the chart and examples of various thoughts and the associated feelings and sensations are below. A blank chart is provided for you to use. You will likely use it any number of times, as you become increasingly aware of the negative thoughts you have and the power of changing them.

What you need

It can be helpful to keep all your notes and homework in one place using a pad or notebook, to see your progress and keep track of what works best for you.

We all have a 'running commentary' in our heads; a stream of thoughts. This is such a universal part of the human experience that we often don't even notice it. It can be quite an eye opener to realise what we've been 'telling ourselves'. It's hard not to believe something we hear over and over. After all, repetition is the cornerstone of successful advertising – and learning because it strengthens the underlying brain circuits as explained further in chapter 2 – How CBT Works.

Just as biologists go out into the wild to observe animals in their natural habitat, you can observe your own thoughts in a scientific manner. You can stop taking them at face value and just notice them. (This is not to negate your common sense. If your thoughts say, for example, 'get out of the way – a car is coming' please listen!)

Write down your observations about your thoughts as you go through your daily activities. It can be quite refreshing and even enlightening to realise what your thinking habits are.

Continue your field study for a few days or more. Note how often specific thoughts (with their associated emotions and sensations) tend to occur.

Use the tables overleaf, or copy them and note:

1. The thought.
2. Circumstances that triggered the thought.
3. Emotions that accompany the thought.

4. Whether the emotions are positive (enjoyable) or negative (unpleasant).
5. Sensations in your body that accompany the thought and/or associated emotions.
6. Frequency – estimate how many times per day or week you have the thought.

The thoughts associated with negative and positive feelings will be used for specific CBT methods described in chapter 5.

Learning how to observe your own thoughts in an unbiased manner is an excellent life skill that will help you notice any developing problems before they interfere too much.

Stigma-busting

If CBT is so great, then why don't more people use it and why is there still so much suffering? Stigma against anything to do with mental health keeps people away from seeking treatment, including CBT.

This stigma comes from the mid-1600s when Western culture took a wrong turn. A man named René Descartes, often called the 'Father of Western Philosophy', convinced everyone that the mind and body are separate (*Meditations on First Philosophy*, 1641). At that time in Western Europe it had been illegal to perform surgery or autopsies because it was believed if you interfered with the body, you interfered with the soul (or mind), and would therefore guarantee the person's eternity in Hell. So in order to allow people to be saved by surgeries, and to allow medical people to learn by examining bodies, Descartes successfully convinced the Church these procedures were okay. But the only way he could do this was to convince everyone that the mind (or soul) and body were separate (also called dualism). He didn't even believe it himself, but could see it would be a helpful idea to break the cultural logjam.

Poor old Descartes would have been horrified to realise the unnecessary suffering he caused. For the next 400 years the physical world, including our bodies, were considered 'real,' whereas our minds were not. This led to the

Chart 1A - Thought Survey - Sample

1	2	3	4	5	6
Thought	Circumstances	Emotions	Positive or Negative (Emotions)	Sensations	Frequency
I'm rubbish.	When I see someone I think is better than me.	Angry, sad, pessimistic.	Negative.	Feel tired, heavy, like it's hard to move.	3 times a day or more.
No one will ever love me.	When I think of asking someone out.	Sad, lonely, empty.	Negative.	Butterflies in stomach, sweaty palms.	1-2 a week.
'You're thick – don't even bother trying'.	When getting a new assignment at work, when I see an interesting book on an unfamiliar topic.	Defeated, tired.	Negative.	Angry, sad, disappointed.	3-5 times a week.
Remembering a great time with a friend.	Seeing someone who reminds me of that friend.	Happy.	Positive.	Feel cheeks pulling up in a smile. Feel warm.	Once a week.
I wonder what it will be like (at this new course, on a new team, having a new flatmate etc).	When starting something new.	Excited, nervous, worried, looking forward to it.	Mixed – both positive and negative.	Sweaty palms, reduced (or increased) appetite.	Once every few months.

Chart 1A - Thought Survey

1	2	3	4	5	6
Thought	Circumstances	Emotions	Positive or Negative (Emotions)	Sensations	Frequency

stigma against anything to do with the mind including mental health. How many times have you heard, 'it's all in your mind', as a way of saying something isn't real?

This idea that the mind and body are separate is wrong, simply not true. Whole new fields of study have blossomed to fill in the gaps science had neglected. It turns out our whole bodies are completely integrated with not only our emotions, but even our thinking about maths and language. Embodied cognition studies find that: posture affects thinking and creativity; children, as well as adults, learn better when they act out their lessons; freezing frown muscles with botox makes it harder to read sad or angry material. See chapter 6 and the book list for more about this topic.

Public efforts to increase access to CBT

CBT is the most frequently recommended talking therapy in the UK and elsewhere. In the UK the National Institute for Clinical Excellence (NICE) guidelines specifies CBT as the first line of treatment for mild depression and a number of anxiety-related problems (http://www.nice.org.uk). Yet only 25% of those suffering with mental health problems in the UK are receiving treatment – mostly medication only (Adult Psychiatric Morbidity Study (APMS), 2007, Information Centre, NHS). Because there are not enough CBT practitioners available to deliver CBT as recommended by NICE, there is an ongoing government programme to train 6,000 additional CBT clinicians by 2015.

Learning happiness in school

Given that 15% of the adults in the UK suffer from common mental disorders (mostly depression and anxiety problems), in 2003 the government started testing a programme based on Martin Seligman's work in 60 English schools. It teaches children CBT techniques to increase their happiness and wellbeing and to give them skills to reduce the likelihood they will suffer from these problems in the future.

Do I need a therapist for CBT?

Like any form of learning, going to a teacher (in this case a therapist) helps. A therapist will have specific skills and knowledge to guide you and help you keep on track. But many studies show that CBT, unlike other forms of talking therapy, can be done effectively using a book like this, and/or augmented by computer-based programs.

Summing Up

- CBT, cognitive behavioural therapy, is the most evidence-based form of talking therapy and has been shown to be effective across all types of mental health problems.
- It works for adults and children, families and couples.
- CBT was born out of observations and research in the 1950s and 60s that revealed the connections between how we think and how we feel.
- Not merely 'thinking positive', CBT is a type of learning from which everyone can benefit, as long as they are willing to do the work that's involved.
- Although there can be benefits of doing CBT along with a therapist, studies show CBT also works when you learn it out of a book, from a computer, or do it in groups. So even if you don't have easy access to a CBT therapist or group, nothing prevents you from going forward and making productive changes for yourself.

Chapter Two

How CBT Works

In this chapter you will learn how CBT uses a number of the brain's natural tendencies. What these tendencies are, and how they work in the brain are explained. Through knowing this, you will be able to start to identify the habits of thought that hold you back. These habits are excellent targets for the CBT methods described in chapters 5-9.

Have you ever travelled your usual route, when you meant to take a different turn? Have you ever caught yourself banging on the 'return' key on the computer like a bongo drum, when part of you realises it didn't work the first time? These are examples of automatic learning.

'Habits are cobwebs at first; cables at last.'

Old Chinese proverb.

Our brains are *always* learning, even when we don't recognise it. When any of these things happen together in time – repeatedly travelling the same route and reaching our destination, hitting the 'return' key and it works – our brains log it and learn it. The brain is like a self-programming computer, and once programmed, it tries to hold on to the information; you need to purposefully work to re-program it. Understanding these natural tendencies of the brain allows you to harness them for your own benefit through CBT.

CBT is learning

CBT is more than just 'thinking positively'. With CBT you're unlearning old, unproductive thinking habits and replacing them with new, productive ones. This is a bit like learning to drive on the right side of the road, after driving on the left for a number of years. This is why CBT works well as you practise the methods. You need to have patience and realistic expectations. Just as you would not expect to play a complicated jazz piece the first time you picked up a saxophone, you need to accept the awkward aspects of this type of learning as well, especially at the start. But if you truly want to change, and you keep trying, you will eventually hit a pure sweet note, and get a taste of what it's like to drive your brain as you choose, rather than it hijacking you.

Our brains are not blank machines, but have a number of abilities and built-in tendencies. One of those abilities is 'associative learning'. This refers to the fact that our brains tend to put things together, or 'associate' them when they occur at the same time.

Accidental learning

'The brain is made up of 100 billion neurons, each making up to 10,000 connections with others. Learning continually remodels these connections throughout our lives.'

Just because two things happen together in time, does *not* necessarily mean one causes the other. But our brains have a tendency to link things that happen at the same time, and to think one causes the other. The more times the two things occur together in time, the stronger your association (learned connection between the two) will be. For example, every time I put the key in my front door, turn it and remove it, the door is locked. I have learned, and completely believe, that turning the key in the door, locks it. In this case it's true that one thing causes the other. But we can also put things together that don't cause each other. For example, I might believe that wearing my lucky socks protects me from asteroids, or that it's necessary to make tomato sauce in a certain order. I may be wrong about both, but unless I try either *not* wearing my lucky socks, or cooking the sauce in a different order, I may never know.

Proportion is king

Our brain works on proportions. These pages look like black ink on white paper, and it would look the same if you were outside in bright sunlight, or reading by a bedside lamp. If our brains worked on absolute values of energy from our senses, indoors the book would look like it was printed on light grey paper, for example, rather than the bright white seen in sunlit conditions. But that's not how the brain works. Proportion is also at work in learning. So if you turn right at the top of your road 98% of the time, you may accidentally do so when you really meant to turn left.

This is important to keep in mind as you do the CBT techniques, because doing things in a new way will often feel awkward and not be very successful at first. You need to do the new ways a number of times before it feels natural. You need to collect more 'ticks on that side of the score sheet' before you and your brain will accept it as normal.

Change reactions

Change can feel awkward. It can be uncomfortable even when changing a habit does *not* create any problems. This is because repetition builds habit and with habit often comes comfort.

Habits can become comfortable because they've become associated with everything being 'okay'. Of course you're not thinking 'the world has not come to an end because I stirred my tea clockwise'. But because the vast majority of the time, everything remains 'just fine' after every cup of tea you make (and you always stir clockwise) then your *brain* may have put these two events together. Hence, the feeling of relief or contentment that comes when the world continues happily on can become associated with your habit, again, without you being aware of learning this on purpose.

This type of accidental association between habits and feelings can be at the heart of anxiety problems including difficulty in social situations, phobias and obsessive-compulsive problems. Undoing this type of accidental learning is key to getting rid of these problems, as explained further in chapters 7 and 9.

Habits can also become comforting when there is a physical rhythm to the behaviour. Research shows that rhythmic behaviours, such as music and knitting, reduce stress levels.

Chart 2A – Change reactions

This exercise lets you sharpen your self-observational skills and lets you increase your tolerance to change. Increasing your ability to weather the feelings of change boosts your power in CBT methods and can help you tolerate or even welcome changes in life more generally.

List two or more things you tend to always do in a certain way or in a certain order. This can be anything from always turning in one direction when you leave your home, always adding your milk and sugar to your tea in a certain order, always stirring it (anti-)clockwise or any other regular habit.

- Column 1: Usual habit.
- Column 2: Does it matter? In this column note if it is possible to do the habit differently without making any undue problems.
- Column 3: Tick when you've tried doing your habit differently
- Column 4: How did you feel when you did it differently?

Chart 2A – Change reactions

Use this chart and make copies.

1 Usual habit	2 Does it matter?	3 Did it differently?	4 How did it feel?

Once you've identified these 'automatically learned habits', do the following experiment. Do each habit differently (where doing so does not put anyone in danger!) and note your reactions in the columns provided. You may be surprised at the thoughts, feelings or sensations you have in reaction to doing things differently.

Brain basis of CBT

Whenever we do something repeatedly, the brain physically strengthens the connections among the underlying brain cells (neurons), whether that's playing the guitar or having negative thoughts about yourself. In this way, your *brain tissue* cannot discern whether or not you're doing something you really want to; it just takes its orders from the fact that you keep doing it! This is a bit like builders carrying out the engineer's plans. The builders (like your brain tissue) are not in a position to question the engineer (you, or your mind).

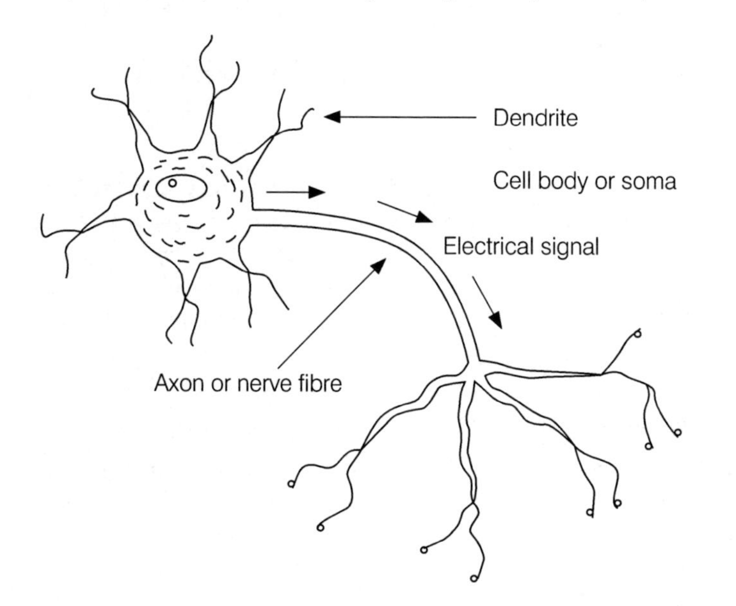

'Neurons communicate with each other through the long thread-like parts. Signals travel across these threads at speeds up to 268 miles per hour.'

Source: Department of Psychology, Stanford University, California.

Neurons are shaped somewhat like starfish, but with much longer, thread-like fibres extending from the centre or body (also called the soma) of the neuron. These fibres branch at their ends as they get near their neighbouring neurons. One longer fibre called the axon generally is the one that carries outgoing signals from the neuron. The axons can be a metre or longer as is the sciatic nerve that runs from the base of our spine to our big toes. Incoming signals to the neuron are carried by shorter fibres called dendrites. Neurons do not touch each other. Signals are transmitted from one neuron to another through chemical signals that travel across the small gaps between neurons called the synapse or synaptic junction. Neurons make these synaptic junctions with each other, with muscles and your internal organs.

Different parts of the brain serve different functions such as: our five (it may be up to 10) senses, language (separate areas for speaking and understanding), maths, music, moving our bodies, emotional attachment to others and different emotions such as sadness and pessimism, optimism and happiness, guilt, anger, anxiety and other functions.

Scientists cannot come to absolute agreement about the human senses. Traditionally, five have been recognised; numbers 6-10 are more recently considered senses as well: 1) sight; 2) hearing; 3) taste; 4) smell; 5) touch; 6) temperature; 7) proprioception (position/movement sensation); 8) pain; 9) balance and 10) acceleration.

The brain is always flexible, responding to how we use it and supporting our habits by strengthening those circuits. With repeated use of any neuronal circuit, the fibres of those neurons develop *more branches* to allow for more connections amongst them. In addition, other neurons will be recruited to join this circuit. It is a myth that we only use 10% of our brain, it's all 'on the job'. When we spend a lot of time doing something, our brains think this is important to us, so that other neurons that had been involved in activities that perhaps weren't quite as critical to us, can be recruited to join this new task.

For example, people who are fluent in more than one language have enlarged language areas of the brain, with subdivisions for each language. If such multilingual people stop speaking one of the languages, their brain reorganises itself again to a smaller area for fewer languages. Professional musicians enlarge the areas of their brains that serve music, and professional perfumers enlarge the areas of the brain discerning scents.

Dr Eleanor Maguire at the University College, London, has been studying London taxicab drivers who take the 3-5 year course called 'the Knowledge' to learn and memorise the entire map of London. Doing the Knowledge, enlarges part of these adults' brains, called the hippocampus. This is the part that records memories and helps with spatial learning (see Dr Maguire's UCL web page for her publications, links and other information: http://www.fil.ion.ucl.ac.uk/Maguire/)

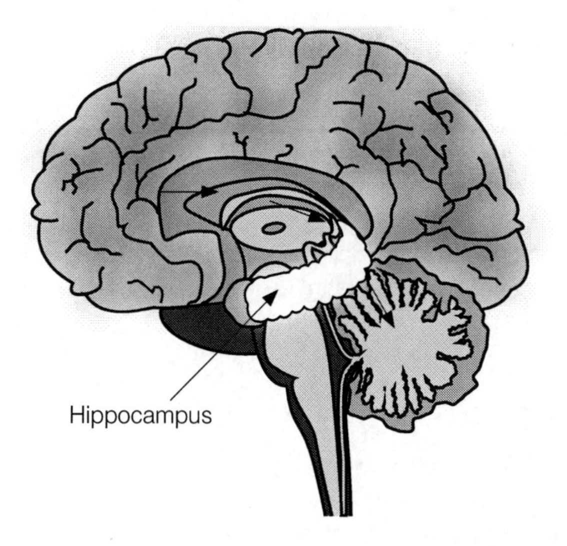

The hippocampus is the part of the brain that makes memories (although they are stored elsewhere) and helps you navigate in the world, including spatial reasoning.

Learning happens when it's 'only' thoughts, emotions and sensations

Brain scanning studies show what sports coaches have known for years – imaginary practice matters. Like slalom skiers practising the course in their mind, to remember the turns and how it should feel. Neural circuits are strengthened even when the practice is done only in our minds with no outward observable behavior. In this way, emotional habits and repetitive thoughts are also learned. The more we practise or do anything, whether it's a foreign language, negative thoughts, or feeling worthless, we learn it – we become virtuosos, even if we don't want to.

Therapy changes the brain

Brain scanning studies show that the talking therapies also change the brain. As these changes are rewarding in and of themselves, we (and our brains) tend to automatically strengthen them. These good changes can persist over time, even after the therapy has ended. It can be difficult to believe in therapy, for the reasons explained in chapter 1 about the history of stigma, but it can also be difficult to relax into the therapy because we have feelings and judgements about how we feel.

Meta-feelings

How often have you heard people say things like, 'I feel stupid for feeling this way, but . . . '? We frequently have emotional reactions to our emotions. You might feel anger, shame or disappointment every time you feel certain emotions. In this way, you may have inadvertently associated your initial feeling with another feeling. These are called 'meta-feelings' meaning feelings about your feelings. They can also be in the form of thoughts, often judgements, but we use the term meta-feelings for expediency and because they tend to have a feeling state with them as well; the distinction between feelings and thoughts can be arbitrary. Even neuroscience tells us they are inextricably woven together.

Banishing meta-feelings is a great way to make inroads into improving your wellbeing. You can also apply the methods in chapters 5 and 7 to meta-feelings. Let yourself feel your feelings without beating yourself up about it! Again, the cultural stigma against emotions and all things of the mind (see section in chapter 1 called Stigma-busting) make it easy for us to think poorly of ourselves for feeling emotions – but please stop. It's healthy to feel our emotions, it's *not* feeling them, pushing them underground that can make us ill – in mind and body.

Chart 2B – Meta-feelings: List reactions you tend to have to specific feelings – things you think, feel or believe about your feelings.

Chart 2B – Meta-feelings

1 Feeling	2 Meta-feeling – your reaction to your feeling

The brain is a processor

In addition to our brain's natural tendency to learn, we also have built-in abilities: for language; to become attached to other people; to experience causation; and to make sense of our sensory information.

Our brains do *not* give us pure information by any means. We do not see the world as a mosaic of different wavelengths of light, but as a meaningful three-dimensional picture. We don't hear groups of sound waves, but voices, cars driving away, doors opening, someone walking toward us. Our brains are prodigious processors and filters of what would otherwise be an overwhelming array of data. Our abilities to process all this information, automatically without us 'lifting a finger', is set up during our development. It is also influenced by our personal histories, expectations, interests and culture. This is described in more detail in chapter 4. For more information on how the brain works see the book list.

Mind-body is one system

The mind and body are *not* separate, but one complexly organised system. Our nervous system is in continual, rich communication with our bodies including all of our internal organs, our immune systems and the rest of our bodies (see chapter 6 for further discussion). The body and the brain use many of the same chemicals to send messages. Emotions typically come with bodily sensations. Changes in appetite and sleep and fatigue are typical symptoms of depression. Most of us will have experienced the butterflies in our stomach or sweaty palms when we get nervous. Often, our physical sensations are the first signs we are feeling stressed, anxious or even depressed.

Physical signals

Sometimes, physical changes are our first indications we're going through some strong emotions. What physical sensations can be telling us and how to harness this information in CBT is discussed in chapter 6.

In chart 2C list any physical signals you've experienced that seem to be related to emotions, and what those emotions might be.

Chart 2C – Physical signals

1 **Physical sign**	2 **Emotion**

Consider the source

It is important to be open to the possibility that the information and feelings we get through our brains may not be the whole story. This requires you to take a balanced approach and to always use common sense (if it's a bus barrelling along – don't question it – jump out of the way!), but we also have to *always* consider that our brains are filters and synthesisers – not merely photocopiers of reality. This is especially important for CBT work; there is a lot of power in *not* necessarily taking our thoughts, feelings and sensations at face value.

Summing Up

- CBT is a form of learning. It utilises the brain's natural tendencies and ways of learning. The brain tends to put things together that happen together in time. It also tends to think one thing causes another (even when it hasn't). Our brains are always doing this – associating things together, learning.
- When we do the same things over and over our brain tissue strengthens this for us, thinking we are trying to learn something. This is true even when the learning involves 'only' thoughts and feelings. This is great when we are, but can also lead to unwanted learning, including having learned negative ideas about ourselves and the world that actually aren't true.
- Once we've 'learned' something, we tend to believe it. CBT identifies those accidentally learned ideas that are making us feel unwell and then shows us how to change it. Brain scanning studies show us that therapy makes changes in the brain – our thoughts are powerful.

Chapter Three

Understanding Yourself

Now that you understand how your thoughts impact you and your brain, you can shepherd them to your advantage. In this chapter you will learn more about yourself. Surveys and inventories will help you identify which thoughts to target. These provide the basis for making the changes you want through the step-by-step methods described in chapters 5-10. These methods will show you how to feel better and enjoy life more, now and into the future.

Negative automatic thoughts – NATs

We now know (chapters 1 and 2) how repetitive negative thoughts affect our wellbeing. How to recognise these negative automatic thoughts (NATs), which often occur in response to specific situations, is the first step. In chapter 5 you are given step-by-step methods for release from what amounts to a 'negative advertising campaigns' against yourself and your mood and wellbeing will improve.

Negative automatic thought (NAT) inventory

Changing NATs is one of the core and most powerful methods in CBT. Once people learn this technique, they tend to use it for the rest of their lives, recognising harmful thinking as it arises and getting rid of it.

What you'll need

Notebook or pad; a copy of the Inventory on page 34; your completed chart 1A from chapter 1, your Thought Survey.

1. NATs. Referring to your thought survey (chart 1A, from chapter 1), look down column 3 (Positive or Negative Emotions) and pick all your thoughts that had negative emotions with them. Enter these in your NAT Inventory on page 34. Listen to yourself. Continue to notice any more NATs and enter them into the Inventory as you become aware of them.
2. Triggers. What are the circumstances when each NAT occurs? When does it occur? Where are you when it tends to happen? And who's around when you tend to have the NAT or are you alone? Note the circumstances, even if there doesn't seem to be any pattern, one may emerge. Triggers may be a thought or feeling as well.
3. Reactions. Note the (3A) Emotions, (3B) Thoughts and (3C) Bodily Sensations that tend to occur along with each NAT. It may be necessary for the NAT to occur a few times before you can make these observations.
4. Scoring. Frequency score: Estimate how often you have each NAT and place the score of 1-3 in column A: Frequency. An approximate estimate is fine.

Frequency score	How often you have the NAT
1	Less than 3 times a day
2	3 to 10 times a day
3	11 or more times a day

Negativity: mild-worst score: Rate each NAT on a scale of 1-10 as to how bothersome, distressing or upsetting you find each one. Your initial 'gut' reaction score is fine. 1 being hardly bothersome or negative at all and 10 being extremely negative. Don't worry about an exact rating, this isn't physics, just your gut reaction as to how unpleasant each NAT is.

In the last column, multiply your scores in column A (frequency) x column B (mild-worst) for a final score for each NAT. This score will be used in guiding you where to start in combating the NATs as explained in chapter 5 – Harnessing Thoughts.

Opposite is an example of a completed NAT Inventory. Only four NATs are used here as an example; typically we all have more.

NAT (Negative Automatic Thought) Inventory Example

1 The NAT	2 Triggers	3 Reactions			4 Scoring		
		3A Emotions	**3B Thoughts**	**3C Sensations**	**4A** Frequency 1-3 (1= Less than 3x per day; 2=3-10 x per day; 3= 11 or more times per day)	**4B** Negativity: Mild (1) to Worst (10)	**4A x B = Score**
'You're an idiot'	When struggling with something at work	Beaten down, anxious,	Who do I think I am? I'm sure to mess this up.	Butterflies in stomach, difficulty swallowing	1	7	7
'I'll never really fit in here'	Someone cancelling social plans with me	Sad, lonely, resentful	It was dumb to think I could move here successfully	Tired, feel heavy	2	5	10
Going over how a social interaction went poorly	Needing to speak to someone new	Nervous, pessimistic	There must be something wrong with me	Sweaty palms	1	3	3
'I hate myself'	Don't seem to be any. Have this a lot.	Sad, angry, pessimistic, resigned	I'm ugly, fat, boring.	Feel like it's hard to move – sluggish, tired	3	10	30

Chart 3A NAT (Negative Automatic Thought) Inventory

The NAT	Triggers	Reactions			Scoring		
		Emotions	Thoughts	Sensations	A Frequency 1-3 (1= Less than 3x per day; 2= 3-10x per day; 3= 11 or more times per day)	B Negativity: Mild (1) to Worst (10)	A x B = Score

You may find it helpful to photocopy the blank inventory for extra copies or draw your own in a notebook or pad. You will use the information you gathered in this inventory in chapter 5, where you are taught methods of stopping the negative and damaging thoughts and replacing them with productive ones.

Who has negative automatic thoughts?

We all have negative thoughts from time to time. They are a lot more frequent and intense in depression, anxiety, stress and post-traumatic stress, eating problems, schizophrenia, bipolar disorder and other problems. For this exercise, it is not necessary to figure out if you have a particular disorder. You can make substantial gains through doing the specific exercises that match your experiences.

Types of negative automatic thoughts

Dr Aaron T Beck (one of the 'fathers of CBT', see chapter 1) and others have found that negative thoughts tend to fall into three categories: about ourselves, our past or our future.

About ourselves:

'I'm useless'; 'You always get it wrong'; 'You don't know what you're doing'; 'I'm fat, ugly, loser, idiot'; or other negative adjectives.

About the past:

'I'm a failure – nothing I've ever done matters'; 'I never should have (married that person/taken that job, etc.)'.

About the future:

'You'll never amount to anything'; 'No one will ever love me'; 'I'll never get a good job'; 'I'm just meant to be everyone's slave'.

'I' versus 'You'. Whenever a NAT is in the third person such as 'You'll never find love', this is a sign that it may be something someone says to you or has said to you in the past. Powerful techniques that diminish NATs related to your history are described in the memory remodelling technique described in chapter 9.

NB: Some people are beset by disturbing thoughts about doing things they know they would never actually do. These thoughts are often about dangerous, hostile, sexual or very unhygienic acts. These thoughts can be hard to resist, and you may find yourself spending so much energy resisting them that it can interfere with your life. If you are having problems with thoughts like these, you may have a type of obsessive-compulsive disorder, or other mental health problem. Chapter 7 explains steps to reduce the power these thoughts have over you, and also guides you to other resources.

Worries

These are usually specific concerns about: things you did in the past and fear they went poorly; or things in the future that you either don't want to happen, or you very much want to happen, but fear they never will.

Worries are a special type of NAT because they can trigger the biology of learning where the brain tissue strengthens the neural circuits. This is because when worry becomes a habit, it can become 'part of the recipe' for doing whatever it is you're worrying about. Let's say you're worried about a meeting with your boss; whether or not your guests will like the meal you've prepared; or if your child will be 'okay' without you at a friend's supervised birthday party. And let's say you then worry about the outcome of the event frequently or even continually until the event ends. Because most of the time things go all right or better, after repeated experiences of 'worry' + acceptable outcome, your brain will pair these two events up as explained in chapter 2. So that after a while of always worrying, and things generally being 'okay', your brain (not 'you') thinks that worry is a necessary ingredient to the process. This is one example of a type of learning called avoidance learning explained in further detail in chapter 7.

These categories of negative thoughts are not mutually exclusive, and any particular NAT or worry you decide to work to reduce may fall into more than one.

Thoughts, emotions and bodily sensations are listed separately to help you see how certain ones tend to 'go together'. After you've filled in your inventory, look down the table and note how many times each type of feeling is engendered. It can be a real eye-opener to see how many thoughts trigger anxiety (worry, trepidation, fear or other related feelings), and what bodily sensations accompany anxiety, such as sweaty palms, shaking, shortness of breath, feeling like you are going to faint, butterflies in the stomach and others.

Once you realise how much time you spend having negative thoughts, you might realise that if you were to do something else – like singing opera – that frequently, you'd be a virtuoso by now.

Judgements

We are often held back by one of two types of judgements: 1) our judging other people; and/or 2) our believing others are judging us.

Judging others

Habitual, negative, judgemental thoughts about others and the world around us, hurts us and our relationships. This is because such thoughts set your expectations about other people and the world, and a wealth of research shows how expectations serve as silent rudders, steering us without our necessarily being aware.

Great expectations

Expectations literally tune our brains by 'changing the filters' on our perceptual processing. What we pay attention to influences and limits the options we see for ourselves and our futures. Having judgemental thoughts on a regular basis such as 'boy, people are idiots', or 'they're doing this on purpose to wind me up (annoy me, etc.)', 'everyone's lazy', and so on, influence our life options in the short and long term.

For example, if you tend to be impatient with other people with accompanying judgemental thoughts, this will show. Your facial expression, tone of voice and body language will broadcast your thoughts. Without a doubt the other person will read these signals. Imagine how that feels to have someone annoyed with you and thinking 'what an idiot', or other negative judgements. This in turn will close down genuine communication and connection, reducing the quality of your immediate interaction and scuppering this relationship and any related future opportunities.

Feeling judged

Many of us are overly concerned about what others think of us. Or more precisely, what *we think others think about us.* This sort of thinking can prevent us from doing things both small and large in our lives, narrowing and lowering the quality of our lives. We can be haunted by self-consciousness about our physical appearance, our accents, or our behaviour. If we're feeling painfully self-conscious, this will also likely show through our facial expression, body language and tone of voice. Once you broadcast how uncomfortable you are, other people will pick this up and react, and you very well may sense they are pulling back in their interaction with you. But it is easy to misinterpret this to mean they are having a negative reaction to you. They're not. They can just see *you're* uncomfortable and are trying not to bother you.

We can also make career, partner and other large life choices based on what we *think* is acceptable, what other people expect of us or what we believe is held in high regard, rather than what we truly want.

It can be hard to tease apart what we truly want from the expectations we've absorbed from family, friends and society more generally. It can take a lot of courage to turn down an esteemed profession for one we feel is less esteemed, but prefer.

Chart 3B – Judgements

The first step in reducing judgements is recognising that we have them or feel them. The chart opposite helps you take stock of any you are experiencing. This information is used in chapter 5, in the section Banishing Judgements, a method to reduce them and the unwanted effects they have on your life.

Column 1 – List judgements.

Column 2 – Are these judgements about others, or judgements you think others are having about you?

Column 3 – List the circumstances when you tend to have them.

Chart 3B – Judgements

1 Judgements	2 About Others, or (you think) About You?	3 Circumstances

Life expectations

Life includes sad, traumatic and distressing events, as well as daily frustrations, annoyances and injustices in the world that should make us angry. CBT does *not* protect you from these, nor should it. Feeling our emotions, including the vagaries of life, is part of living and necessary for keeping healthy. Denying our feelings is unhealthy and leads to mental and physical health problems in the long term. It is when sadness doesn't fade, anger bubbles up at minor events or worries or other negative thoughts and feelings interfere with our daily life, that CBT is appropriate.

It is not always easy to know when ordinary, healthy emotions are taking root in unhealthy ways. Use your common sense; ask yourself if this was happening to someone else, would you think the emotions, thoughts or behaviours were out of balance? Ask others, including people whose opinion you respect, and there is always professional help out there (see the help section).

When to seek assistance

Such is the human condition that we all will experience symptoms that come under the titles of any number of mental disorders. This does not necessarily mean we have the disorder, but that we are part of humanity. If you find that your emotions, thoughts or behaviours are interfering with your work and/or social and family life, then why not seek professional advice and feel better sooner? See chapter 10 and the help list at the end of the book.

Summing Up

- In this chapter you did an inventory of thoughts that are the best targets for the CBT methods described in the following chapters.
- Decades of research shows that reducing negative automatic thoughts (NATs) is a powerful way to diminish depression and anxiety.
- NATs tend to be about: ourselves, our future or past, or be in the form of worries.
- Judgements about others, or thinking others are judging us is another type of negative thought that commonly holds us back.
- CBT is a methodology for living life healthily and fully. But it is not, nor is it meant to be, protection from life and its vagaries.

Chapter Four

Freedom From Your Past – and Present

How we become ourselves

'Nature or nurture?' is no longer a meaningful question – human development is both; the two influences are inextricably intertwined. It's like asking how a plant would grow without sun, soil and rain, or if it was in a shed with only a slice of light coming through. Our development is driven by the stimulation in our environments; so, too, are our adult lives maintained and continuously impacted.

'Did you know a baby is born with the ability to speak Mandarin?'

When we're born, every brain system – vision, hearing, movement, taste, language and emotion – is poised to unfold in response to the world. This is also true for bodily systems such as the immune system and the functions of the internal organs.

The environment profoundly impacts the development of our nervous systems. For example, all babies across the globe make all of the sounds found in all the world's languages. But as we grow up speaking the language(s) spoken to us, we actually lose the ability to make and even hear some of the other sounds that are not used in our first language(s). This is why it can be so hard to learn and speak another language properly when we're older.

If an infant's eyes are occluded, by cataracts, for example (an unwanted side effect from the 100% oxygen given to premature infants in decades past), and this is not corrected by age 7, the adult, like the plant in that poorly lighted shed, will be largely or wholly blind because the visual system in the brain did not get enough stimulation to develop properly. When these children had their cataracts removed in adulthood, they saw only blotches of colour and light, but could not resolve a meaningful three-dimensional world; that developmental window had been closed. Often they reverted to being blind because their brains shut off the visual cacophony because it was more confusing than helpful.

Emotional development drives brain development

We develop and learn emotions in the same way we develop language, vision or walking. In fact, the emotional system drives and organises the brain's overall early development. Our very survival depends on these early emotional bonds. Severe emotional neglect – even with adequate food and physical care – can cause changes in the chemical systems of the brain and body. Denied emotional bonding, a child's brain will stop secreting growth hormone from the pituitary gland. Children with this medically recognised condition (psychosocial dwarfism or psychosocial short stature) will stop gaining weight even though they are eating and their growth may be stunted. Without intervention, some of these children will die – from a lack of emotional connection.

Hence, the emotional attachment system, or simply 'attachment', is the single most important system in the brain at birth. As infants we are primed to bond with no more than three other humans. These emotional bonds drive brain development through a structure called the Amygdala.

The Amygdala: The Mediator

Emotional learning occurs in a pair of almond-shaped structures, located near each hippocampus (in the temporal lobes). The amygdalae mediate the interaction between emotional attachment and brain development. For example, specific neurons in the amygdala will die if an infant does not get enough eye contact during the first few months of life. If these neurons survive, they then carry on and make connections to other brain areas. If they die, this profoundly impacts social behaviours, and the ability to remember faces, for the rest of the person's life.

NB: Babies are very resilient. The *lack* of eye contact necessary to kill off these special amygdala neurons is profound. Even if you had difficulty bonding with your infant, or suffered postnatal depression, if your baby's other developmental milestones were within normal range, you can be assured they did get sufficient eye contact.

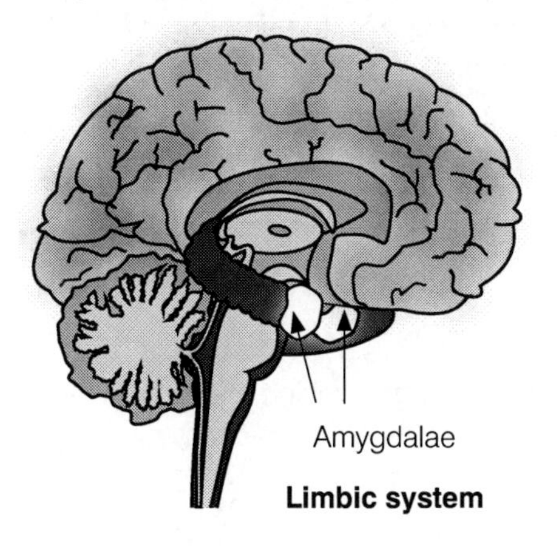

The amygdala is also involved in fear and rage reactions and remains central in our emotional reactions and learning throughout our lives. Often it is this early learning through the amygdalae that sets up trigger reactions in adults, reactions that can be out of proportion and hard to understand in terms of the current circumstances. More about how these triggers work in the brain and how to diffuse them is explained in chapter 8.

The amygdala is a paired structure (white). It is located at the end of, and is highly connected to the hippocampus which is also on both sides of the brain (the larger C-shaped dark grey structure).

Long-term impact

Just as we learn to hear and speak the sounds of our first language without being aware of the options when we're young, we also learn our emotions. Our early attachment experience sets up our emotions for life. The emotions we feel, in what proportions and in what circumstances, the relationships we're drawn to, how we react and much more, are all guided and imprinted by this early emotional learning. This learning tends to be invisible to us, it's 'just how we feel and how we are' – until we look at it.

Narrative style survey

Research shows that our narrative style as adults (how we tell fictional or non-fictional stories) reflects our early attachment experience as babies and children. This may sound far-fetched, but try the quiz below and see for yourself. Once we understand a bit about how central the emotional development is to overall brain development, it's not such a surprise.

Which of the story-telling styles described below do you tend to use? Decide for yourself and ask someone else who will tell you the truth. Then decide what the best answer is and write it in column 3 – Consensus opinion.

Narrative styles

1. Very organised – usually tell a story with a clear storyline and a beginning, middle and end.
2. Mostly organised – may wander off course a bit, but usually catch this yourself and return to an organised narrative.
3. Meandering-completer – go off on tangents but you do eventually come back and finish the story. Sometimes you need to be prompted by others to return to the story.
4. Meandering-wanderer – go off on tangents without feeling the need to come back to the original story.
5. Very brief storyteller – only if you are forced and you tend to give a very quick overview.

Narrative style survey

1 Your opinion	2 Someone else's opinion	3 Consensus opinion

Narrative style – Key

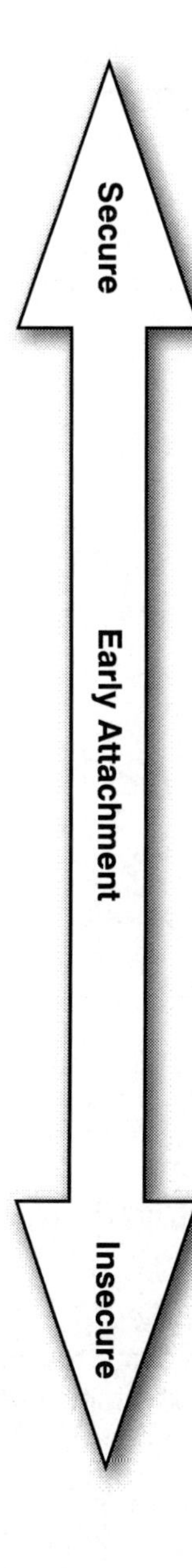

Very organised: Secure Attachment
You had a very good or adequate early attachment. The adults who raised you were consistent, dependable and balanced towards your needs. You felt loved and could take it for granted. Your adult relationships likely are balanced, secure, dependable and largely healthy.

Mostly organised: Fairly Secure Attachment
Your early attachment was largely consistent, dependable and balanced in responding to your needs. You were loved and knew it, yet there were also a certain amount of times when the adults could not respond to you in a balanced way. Your adult relationships will be mostly balanced and secure, but you may also be drawn to relationships where your partner is somewhat inconsistent toward you.

Meandering-completer: Mixed Secure and Insecure Attachment
Your early attachment was an approximately even mixture of dependable and consistent, as well as unpredictable and unresponsive toward your needs. You will likely feel conflicted about your adult attachments, possibly always questioning your relationships. You may have difficulty finding steady relationships and either feel stifled or insecure in them.

Meandering-wanderer: Mixed/Conflicted Secure & Insecure Attachment
There was a considerable lack of balanced response to you and your needs as a child. You could not count on the adults being 'there' for you or on your side. You got love as a child, but may have had to work very hard for it. You may latch on to relationships in adulthood, even when they are not that good, or have a number of difficult ones.

Very brief: Insecure Attachment
Your carers were largely unable and/or dysfunctional in their bond with you. They may have been largely absent, non-interactive or you might have suffered maltreatment. You may have had significant disruptions in your early relationships. Adult relationships may replay the style of bonding you experienced as a child. If this was maltreatment, then you might find you end up in abusive relationships. This is a vulnerability, but not a destiny.

Attachment legacy

The 'emotional grammar' woven in through our development plays out in many, if not all, aspects of our lives as adults; in our relationships with others, with ourselves and with our work.

We are all impacted by the style, dynamics and qualities of our early relationships. This varies from the optimal impact of healthy, loving and adequate early attachment, to wholly inadequate early attachments. Most of us experience something in-between: a mixed early attachment, with aspects that supported and nourished our development and aspects that hindered or interfered. Inadequate early attachments can be due to neglect, witnessing violence, changes in who raises the child, and maltreatment including physical, sexual and psychological. The wounds left by maltreatment are more related to the quality of the relationships available to the child, than to the type of abuse. Studies at Harvard University have found that profound neglect has a greater effect on the brains of boys than sexual abuse. We all exist somewhere along this continuum.

Continuum of the quality of our early attachment experience

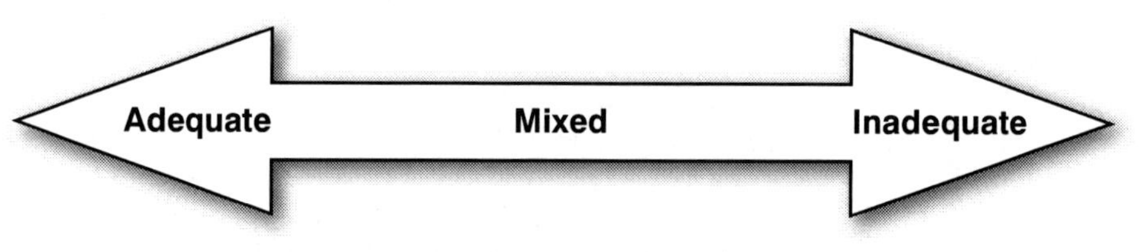

The power of knowing

Why worry about what happened in our childhoods all those years ago? Isn't this blaming our parents for our problems?

It's not a matter of blaming, it's a matter of understanding so we can stop patterns we didn't start, but that are steering our lives, sometimes in directions we don't want. These patterns go across generations. Most mental health problems are due more to these transgenerational attachment legacies, than to genes.

Emotional memories

But how can this early brain development affect us so much in the present if we don't even remember it?

You may not remember, but your body and brain do. There are three reasons we often don't remember things consciously, even emotionally potent events. 1) Emotion associated with events is recorded with greater strength in the brain, compared to the facts of the memory – who, what, when, where (see chapter 7 for more information). 2) Emotional memories and learning start within months of birth as the amygdala responds to our first emotional bonding, whereas permanent factual memories don't begin until the ages of 2½-5 years old, on average, coinciding with the hippocampus fibres reaching their target. 3) At times, to protect us, our brains block trauma. Yet research shows that the nervous and bodily systems of those of us with maltreatment histories, respond differently long after the maltreatment ended. Our biology doesn't forget.

Maltreatment – a global concern

25-50% of all children across the world have been physically abused. *World Health Organisation, child maltreatment, fact sheet No 150, August 2010.*

20% of women and 5-10% of men report being sexually abused as children. *World Health Organisation, child maltreatment, fact sheet No 150, August 2010.*

Maltreatment at any time during a lifespan increases rates of depressive and anxiety symptoms; the risk of an addictive disorder; and the chances you will suffer post-traumatic stress disorder, if you are subjected to additional trauma later on.

In the UK 25.3% of those aged 18-24 were severely maltreated during childhood. *National Society for the Prevention of Cruelty to Children, child abuse and neglect in the UK today, 2011.*

The brain bounces back

But all is not gloom and doom. Although our brains develop at a steep rate after birth, continuing until we are about 27 years old, further learning, including refinement and change in our brain connections continues throughout our lives including into older age.

It also transpires that we get about 1,500 new neurons *each day,* throughout adulthood. Many of these are born into the limbic circuits – involved with emotions and memories, hence a real opportunity for change.

CBT is for leaving the past behind

'Is the biology of depression the biology of early trauma?'

At the 2002 American Psychiatric Association's annual meeting, Charles Nemeroff MD, PhD of Emory University asked his audience.

With your new knowledge of development, you now have an understanding of your own, and other's behaviour. Although there are some universal patterns that help shed light on the connection between past and present, the details of how your past impacts your present are infinitely varied across humanity. Most of us have some aspects of the different situations below.

Negative automatic thoughts in the third person

If you have a lot of negative automatic thoughts, and/or if some of them occur in the third person as in, 'You'll never amount to anything', you likely received or heard considerable negative messages when you were young. This could have reflected how the adults who cared for you felt about themselves, which in turn would have been impacted by their early attachment. See chapter 5 on how to combat these negative thoughts to improve your mood.

High levels of anxiety

If you have high levels of anxiety or worry, you may have experienced a considerably unpredictable early emotional environment. The mood of your parents/carers could have been hard to predict or you may have experienced considerable disruption in your attachments through a change in parents/ carers. See chapter 7 for methods to harness anxiety.

Can't say no?

If you have difficulty saying 'no' to others, and are always doing everything for everyone, you may have been in the role of being a support or help to the adults in your childhood, more than would have been optimal. See chapter 8 for methods to balance this.

Anger problems

People who have a 'short fuse', pop off in anger or rage with insignificant provocation, often had something go a bit (or a lot) wrong in their attachment before the age of 5. It could be that the early bonding during infancy was inadequate or that the parent was unable to bond as well with the child as they left infancy and became more independent. See chapter 9 for successful methods to tame your reactions to triggers.

CBT can be an important part of healing from such a past or present as it can help reduce the many different negative feelings that often continue, even after the trauma has stopped. In addition to CBT techniques, telling your story and being heard can also be an immeasurable help. We are intrinsically social animals. Just as our early survival depends on it, we are no less impacted and dependent on social interaction as adults as discussed further in chapter 10. Being heard and understood by another person is central to being human and key to talking therapy. And for any of us who have not been heard well enough in the past, therapy can help us catch up in this need. Being fully heard also helps you listen to yourself. Resources for finding a suitable professional to speak with, as well as books and online resources are listed in the help section.

'In the US, 23.6% women and 11.5% men have been victims of domestic violence.'

US Centers for Disease Control and Prevention. February 8, 2008.

Summing Up

- Our early brain development is driven by our earliest emotional bonds.
- Without sufficient eye contact, specific brain cells die, and without sufficient bonding, a child can die despite physical care.
- In addition to the legacy early maltreatment leaves us to heal, we all are bequeathed the imprint of our early emotional bonds and learning. Once we recognise those aspects of our development, we can discern what is truly part of us, and what is part of a behavioural pattern that in reality came to us across the generations. With that knowledge comes the strength to do the work to change.

Chapter Five

Harnessing Thoughts

Because of the brain tissue's habit of strengthening anything we do repeatedly, unchecked negative thoughts are further strengthened every time we indulge them. Remember, if you were to practise the guitar as often as you think negative thoughts or worry, you might be touring the world by now.

Using the following methods, you can eradicate these negative thoughts and worries. Diminishing what amounts to a 'negative advertising campaign' against yourself has real power to change your mood state and general experience of the world. This will have a good 'domino effect' in your life. When you're using enjoyable brain circuits your facial expression and body language will reflect this, compared to if you were engrossed in dark, negative, pessimistic ones. Your changed expressions will draw different people to you, and people will also react to you differently. With improved emotional states, you will see opportunities you hadn't noticed before, and over time see changes in your personal, social and work life.

'If I make dark my countenance, I shut my life from happier chance.'

Alfred Lord Tennyson, *The Two Voices.*

Here you are taught three powerful techniques: 1) Thought replacement; 2) Banishing judgements; and 3) Worry appointments. Once you learn these core techniques you can adapt them for numerous types of unwanted and unproductive thoughts that we all get stuck on from time to time. These are core tools to be used as suits.

Technique 1: Thought replacement

Overview

Thought replacement is a core CBT technique applicable and adaptable to many situations. In thought replacement you 'boss back' any unwanted or negative automatic thought (NAT) and then think a really pleasant thought instead. The really pleasant thought is one you've picked from a real life memory and practised beforehand, so you have it ready and it has some strength. These pleasant thoughts are called vivid pleasant moments (VPMs). This is doubly powerful. First, it stops you from further strengthening the brain circuits underlying the negative thoughts, while also strengthening circuits that underlie pleasant ones. This allows you to get the reins of your brain back in your own hands. Whereas it can feel like your thoughts are 'hijacked' to the negative ones, thought replacement gives you practice in engaging much more pleasant and productive parts of your brain. After all, we're all capable of thinking a seemingly infinite variety of thoughts – why not choose enjoyable and productive ones, rather than living in the dungeons many of our brains can also create.

There are two steps to thought replacement: a 'preparation stage'; and then the 'practice phase'. The practice phase becomes your new way of doing things, until that particular NAT leaves you alone, at which time you can apply it to the next one you decide to banish.

Step 1 – Preparation stage

Choosing a vivid pleasant moment

You need to choose and then practise the vivid pleasant moment first, before substituting it for the negative thought. This is because those negative thoughts can be hard to shake, so you need to have something of real strength to compete. Funny, non-serious moments often make the best VPMs. Times when you remember being completely 'stuck in', engrossed in a pleasant situation. *Avoid* memories that include pain, trauma, sad or difficult relationships. For example, giving birth and big momentous occasions generally do *not* make good VPMs. Better types of choices are remembering dancing with your niece on your toes, giggling with a loved one, friend or even a stranger. Or a funny interaction with an animal. Pick something you would *like* to relive any number of times!

Practise your vivid pleasant moment twice a day for 3-5 days

Pick times of day for regular practice, for example while you're on the bus to work or in the evening after dinner. You can also practise bringing up this moment when you have some spare time such as waiting in queue. Remember your pleasant moment as a vivid daydream. Bring in all your senses and 'replay' the 'movie' in your mind. Were you outside or inside? Cold or warm? Was there a breeze? What did you see all around you? What did you hear? What did you smell, taste or feel? Make appointments with yourself to practise.

Continue your twice daily (or more) practice of your VPM for approximately 3-5 days, or until you can bring it up and re-experience it immediately and fully at will.

Sensory signal

Some people find it helpful to use a sensory trigger to help invoke the VPM such as tapping yourself on your hand, turning a ring on your finger and the like. This is an option but not necessary.

Why pick just one VPM?

It's important to start with only one VPM because you will use this to substitute for the negative thoughts and at that time you do not want to be trying to decide which one to use. If you dally there trying to decide, the NAT will have a chance to sneak in and take hold.

Negative automatic thought worksheet

Using your negative automatic thought inventory from chapter 3, enter your NATs in the worksheet overleaf along with the scores from the inventory. Now rank them from lowest to highest score. Give the NAT(s) with the lowest score a ranking of '1' the next lowest '2' and so on. If two or more NATs have the same score, give them the same ranking. If you have 8 NATs all with different scores, then you will have a ranking of 1-8. If you have 8 NATs, but two have the same score, then you will have a ranking of 1-7, with two NATs having the same ranking. See the example below.

NAT worksheet example

Transfer your NATs and scores from the inventory in chapter 3. Rank them from lowest to highest, giving the least compelling one a rank of '1'. Any ties get the same rank as in the example overleaf.

Negative automatic thought (NAT)	Score (From your NAT Inventory, Chapter 3)	Rank
No one's ever going to love me.	60	5
I'm an idiot.	75	6
You got it wrong, again!	25	3
Everyone thinks you're weird.	12	1
They're talking about me.	22	2
I'll never get a good job.	42	4
I'm ugly.	22	2

Chart 5A NAT worksheet

Use this worksheet, or make your own and fill it in as described above.

Negative automatic thought (NAT)	Score (From your NAT Inventory, Chapter 3)	Rank

Step 2 – Practice phase

Start with your NAT with the lowest score

Like any type of learning, you start with the easier parts first. Generally the higher the NAT's score (frequency rating x negativity rating), the more challenging it is to defeat. So we start with the easier ones to shift. Like learning to play the piano, you don't start with a Beethoven piano sonata or playing in a competition – you start with Twinkle, Twinkle Little Star – simple exercises and songs!

Boss back your negative thought (NAT) and substitute your very pleasant moment (VPM)

Whenever the NAT arises, boss it back and substitute the VPM. Jump into your VPM at the first sign of your NAT. Don't worry if it's awkward and only partially successful at first – NATs are tenacious! You may find you have an argument in your head with your NAT where you keep 'telling it' to buzz off, but 'it' keeps coming back. You may find yourself having 'Yes, but', conversations in your head with the NAT trying to come back in. Just keep practising *bossing back the NAT and substituting the VPM*. Like learning how to serve a tennis ball, lay bricks or make a perfect meringue, the first tries are often inglorious and clumsy. But the brain is a tremendous machine of intent. If you keep trying and you want to learn this, you will. It is worth the work, as this technique will be useful for the rest of your life.

Step 3 – 'Wash, rinse, repeat'

Continue practising the thought replacement until the NAT stops occurring. After you've banished the first one, apply the thought replacement to your NAT with the next lowest score, and so on.

Top-ups

NATs are stubborn and even after getting rid of any specific one, it may return occasionally. Don't worry. This is normal and not a sign that you've failed in any way. The more you let the circuits underlying the NAT go fallow, the less strength they have over time, although they may spark up occasionally, especially in times of stress or hardship. Once you've had the practice of banishing it the first time round, *if* it returns, it tends to be much weaker and you may even find that although you notice it, it no longer has the same negative power over you. For any recurrence, just re-engage the thought replacement method to get rid of these last remnants. Many NATs will completely stop on a permanent basis.

Technique 2: Banishing judgements

Overview

Habitually having negative thoughts about others and the world at large or worrying what others think of you, will also influence your thinking and expectations – you'll will start to believe them! In addition, your thoughts will show in your facial expression and body language, at least to some extent – so others *will* know 'what you're thinking'. The reality of any given situation is usually more complex than our sweeping, negative judgements would indicate. Judgements are like blinkers on a horse – they narrow our view, robbing us of the real options.

'By not caring too much about what people think, I'm able to think for myself and propagate ideas which are very often unpopular. And I succeed.'

Albert Ellis.

Banishing judgement method

This technique allows you to stop assuming you're right about other people. 'Judgement' is used here to include both your judgements about other people and what you think they might be thinking about you.

Column 1: Take your judgements from your inventory in chapter 3 and write them down in the column 1 in chart 5B below

Column 2: Write what might also be going on *with the other person*, rather than what your judgement would indicate.

Column 3: Write an alternate thought you could have in that situation. This can be about anything. Try asking yourself questions about the immediate environment or situation; for example, use your senses to notice your surroundings.

Column 4: How might you find out if the other person really is acting a certain way on purpose or having certain thoughts about you? Could you ask them how they're feeling, because maybe their odd facial expression is *not* a comment on you, but indication they're not feeling well. If you think people giggling together are laughing at you, could you walk by them (getting a cup of tea perhaps) and join in the conversation in a friendly way? Usually, people are not talking or thinking about any one of us as much as we may think they are.

Chart 5B Judgement Restructuring

1 Judgement	2 What *else* might be going on?	3 Alternative thought	4 How to check

Rehearsal

Imagine a typical scenario for the first judgement on your list. Then *say aloud* your alternate thought, rather than your usual judgement. Saying the alternate thought aloud helps you learn it more quickly because you are using more than one modality: you're thinking *and* hearing it.

Repeat this exercise for each of your typical judgements.

Practice

Next time you find yourself in a situation where one of your judgements occurs, quickly replace it in your thoughts with your alternate thought. *Do this even if you don't yet believe your alternate thought and have trouble not believing your judgement.* Remember, your poor brain has been subjected to these judgements for a long time, probably years. The very repetition itself, becomes convincing even if it isn't true as explained in chapter 2.

N.B. If you have difficulty taking reassurance that others are *not* talking about you or otherwise interfering with you (your email, computer or other private material), and if some of your concerns start to include worries about organised efforts to intrude or hassle you, then you may be having paranoia. If you are, it can be a symptom of a serious, biologically driven brain disorder and you should seek help. Ask your GP for a referral.

Technique 3: Worry appointments

Overview

It can be very hard to stop worrying. Like any other repeated activity of the mind, worrying can also trigger the brain to strengthen the underlying circuits, making you even 'better' at worrying. There is more about this in chapter 2 on how CBT works (see Accidental Learning) and chapter 7 Emotional Logic. For some of us worry can spiral out of control so that we find ourselves finding something to worry about even when we've run out of things!

Getting the reins of your brain back into your hands for worrying can be done using 'worry appointments', which you can also modify and use for other unwanted thoughts as well.

Chart 5C Worries to banish chart

Write down the worries you have. Then rate them as follows:

1. Very mild, can mostly or almost ignore.
2. Mild but harder to ignore.
3. Somewhat bothersome.
4. Quite bothersome and difficult to ignore.
5. Very bothersome and impossible to ignore.

Worry	Rating Scale 1 (very mild) – 5 (very bothersome)

Worry appointment procedure

Five-minute appointments:

When the worry hits you, tell yourself you can worry about this, *but in five minutes.* While you're 'waiting for your appointment' try to get involved in something else, work, reading, your phone, computer or any other distraction or productive endeavour. Even if you do nothing but watch the clock for five minutes while saying to yourself, 'I've got to wait, can't worry yet', and the like, that is fine. Just do your best to put it off until the appointed time. When the time comes, worry as hard as you can for 90 seconds. You may be surprised at how long 90 seconds can seem. At the end of your 90 seconds, push the worry away again.

- If at the appointment time you no longer feel like worrying, *great!* In this case, please do *not* worry!
- If you forget your appointment, having become engrossed in something else, this is also a good outcome.
- Repeat this procedure every time the worry returns.

Longer appointments

After mastering five-minute worry appointments, extend for longer periods of time. For example, 10, 20, and then 30-minute appointments. This is a guide only and you can time them as works best for you.

Follow the same procedures so that when the appointment time comes, if you can put it off again, or decide not to do your 90 seconds of worrying at all, that's terrific. And if you forget the appointment all together, better yet!

Daily appointments

As you get more and more skilled at the worry appointments, some people find it useful to make a daily worry appointment where they do all the worrying for the day. Usually at the end of the day is best. You schedule a 15-minute slot when you sit down (maybe with a cup of relaxing herbal tea) and go through all the things you usually worry about. When worries come up during the day, you remind yourself that you will have time to think about it at your appointment time.

Thinking appointments

None of us get enough time to think. This can be one reason worries grab us. As you become more proficient with your worry appointments, you may find that your daily appointments turn into thinking appointments rather than worry appointments. This is great, and a very healthy habit to cultivate.

Invent your own methods

All the CBT methods can be modified to suit your needs. Please apply them to any and all situations where you find you've gotten a bit stuck thinking unproductively, even if it's a one-off situation. Do not worry about fitting into any neat description of a NAT, worry or judgement. You can evoke your very pleasant moment any time you want to shift your mood. And of course you can invent your own methods of shepherding your brain activity into more pleasant and productive circuits.

Summing Up

In this chapter you were given step-by-step instructions for three core CBT techniques: Through replacement; banishing judgements; and worry appointments. All of these methods are based on:

- Recognising the unproductive, negative and otherwise harmful thoughts.
- Developing means to think it less often whether that's by putting it off (as in the worry appointments), or substituting a more productive thought (as in the thought replacement and banishing judgements).
- Increasing your time spent using pleasant and productive brain circuits – why not strengthen these!

Chapter Six

Mind Field

Emotions are information

How many of us think that emotions are a sign of weakness, something to be batted away or ignored? That rational thought is king, that decisions should be based on logic? Neuroscience research reveals that emotions are essential and anatomically intertwined with rational thinking, as are our bodily sensations. Our minds arise from this field of data.

'Emotions and the feelings are not a luxury, they are a means of communicating our state of mind to others. But they are also a way of guiding our own judgments and decisions. Emotions bring the body into the loop of reason.'

Antonio Damasio.

Mapping emotions

Research on how we experience emotions generally finds three characteristics:

1. There are recognisably different emotions (it's not just one big emotion that we feel).
2. Some emotions seem to be the opposites of others (for example joy compared to sadness in Robert Plutchik's scheme reprinted overleaf).
3. Emotions can be further refined to more detailed levels. For example, love can be further divided into affection, longing, lust, adoration and other forms, as detailed in Professor W. Gerrod Parrott's tree-like scheme (see book list).

Robert Plutchik's Wheel of Emotions

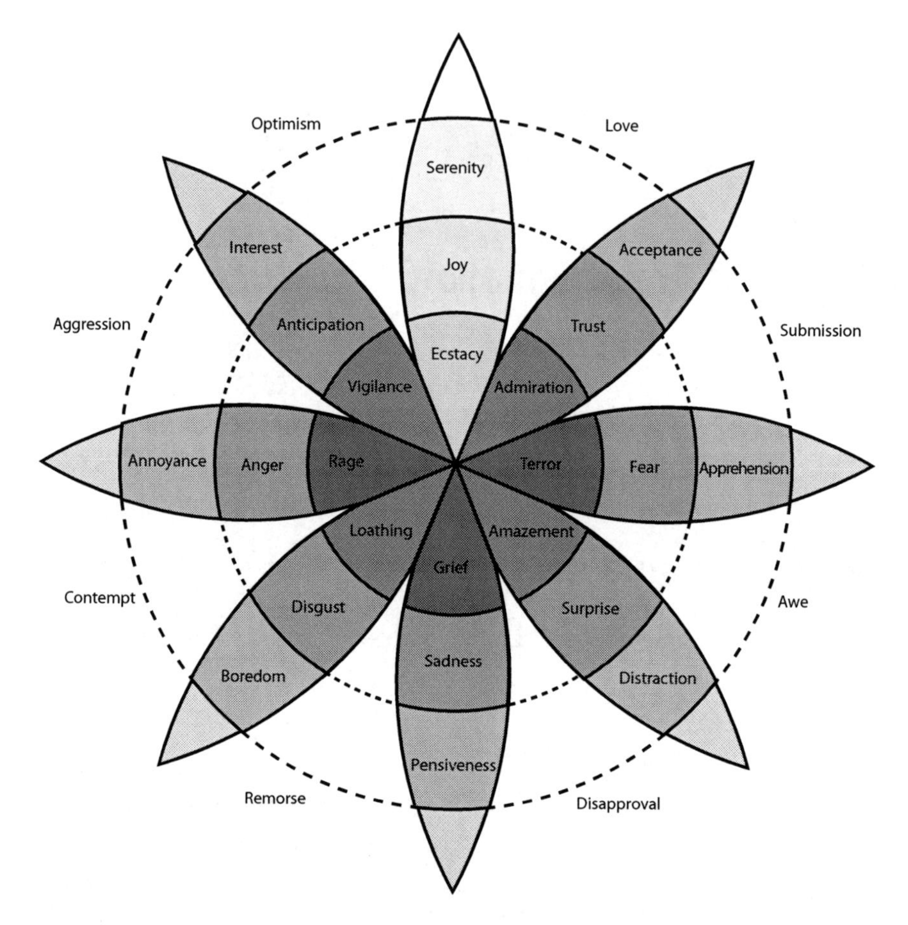

Robert Plutchik had a long career in psychology research with a focus on emotions. His *Wheel of Emotions*, published in 1980, is still used today. It consists of 8 basic emotions (sadness, surprise, fear, trust, joy, anticipation, anger and disgust). The advanced emotions outside the rings, are considered to be combinations of the two basic emotions nearest to it (remorse as a combination of disgust and sadness for example).

Mind field

We now know that 'mind' does not solely happen in the brain, but comes from a field of information including our bodies. These connections are studied in a field called embodied cognition (see the book list). We monitor our bodies including our heart and other internal organs in a part of the brain called the insular cortex. Our body awareness is used to interpret the information our senses give us; our emotions are a result of the synthesis of this information.

People vary in how good they are at perceiving their bodily signals, called interoception. Those who are better at it are less likely to be tricked by illusions and are more confident about their intuitions. 'Gut feelings', and 'following your heart' may be real, after all. But researchers, Barnaby Dunn at the Cognition and Brain Sciences Unit in Cambridge, UK, found that being confident in intuitions was *not* necessarily related to being right!

Increasing interoception exercise

Like all other skills, interoception can be increased and there is reason to think doing so will increase emotional intelligence. Try this exercise at least three times a week for a minimum of two weeks. Keep track of your data each time you do it, to monitor progress in chart 6A overleaf.

1. Sit down in a quiet place (even quietly ticking clocks can interfere with this exercise).
2. Mentally estimate your pulse for 10 seconds and multiply by 6 for your pulse in beats per minute. Do not feel your pulse with your fingers – you're trying to see how well your brain monitors this. Don't worry about how to do this, just try – even guess at first. Be careful not to stare at a clock with a sweep hand that moves with each second, as you can accidentally count this instead. Record your mental estimate in column 2 overleaf.
3. Measure your pulse for 10 seconds and multiply by 6 to get your rate per minute. There are two ways to measure your pulse.

   a. **Radial-Wrist pulse.** Place one hand palm side up. Place the index and middle fingers of your other hand on your wrist, about 2-3cm below the base of the hand and press in gently between your outer bone and middle tendon until you feel a throbbing – your pulse.

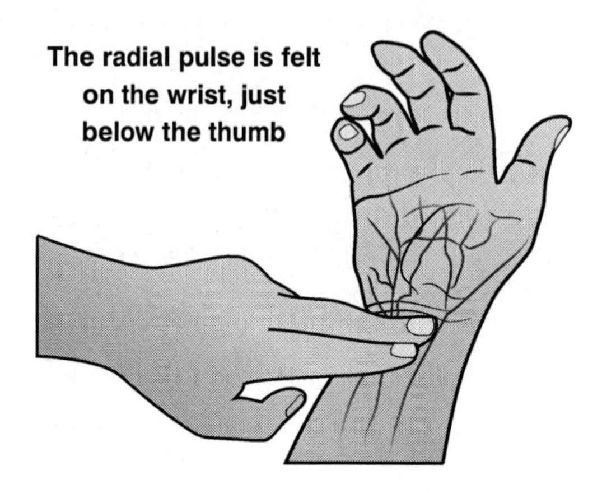

b. **Carotid-Neck pulse.** Place the index and middle fingertips (from one hand) gently on your neck, midway between your neck muscles and windpipe until you find your pulse.

Record your measured pulse in column 3.

In column 4 note your stress level from 0 (none) to 5 (maximum) at the time.

In column 5 note your mood around the time of your pulse measurements.

Chart 6A – Interoception practice

Use this chart and/or make your own copies for more observations.

1 Date	2 Mental Estimate of Pulse	3 Measured Pulse	4 Stress level 0 – 5	5 Mood state

Over time you should get better at estimating your pulse, even if you are not aware of how you are doing it (the brain responds to your intentions and there are many brain processes of which we are not aware). You may find that better interoception is associated with certain moods or stress levels. This exercise serves two purposes: 1) It shows you how your perception of your body is related to mood state; and 2) Improving interoception, over time, will help you be more aware of your true emotions as well.

Looking for answers

Research shows that our brains are primed to find reasons for our feelings, even when they're physically caused. For example, classic studies found that if people are given adrenalin without their knowing it, they will attribute the resulting physical experience to psychological nervousness when presented with an ambiguous stimulus. (In this case, a researcher in the white coat who walks through, but says nothing). People who were given a sugar pill didn't find this same white-coated man ominous.

Emotions can come from 'the inside-out', when you're thinking about something, or the 'outside-in'. (For example, when you see your best friend unexpectedly). Even purely mechanical influences on our expression of emotion can influence how we process emotion – like smiling making us feel brighter. When people were given botox to freeze their frown muscles, it took them longer to read (to themselves) sad or angry sentences. Emotions also are affected by learning, cultural and social influences.

Emotion survey

Perceiving our emotions – being aware of them – is the first and necessary step to knowing how to handle them.

It is unfelt emotions that hurt us. Hiding, denying or in any other way forcing our emotions away so we don't feel them, leads to health problems – of body and mind.

Like learning music, language, maths and all other skills, we can also become better at perceiving our emotions.

Chart 6B Emotion survey

As you notice your emotions, note down the following:

1. The emotion.
2. Circumstances when you have it.
3. How you express it. If you don't express it at all, put a '0' in this column. If you act differently or opposite to how you feel, then note this down.

   a. Ask someone who knows you well, what emotions they think you're feeling under different circumstances. Most of us are worse actors than we think. You can try to cover your real feelings with words, but body language and facial expression are harder to control. This is healthy; it's when we completely squash our true feelings that we have problems long term. But you may want to try another manner of responding to the emotions that are coming through when you think you've hidden them. Because this will also come through – the fact that you are trying to conceal them, albeit unsuccessfully.
4. Is it comfortable or unpleasant on a scale of 1-5, where 1 is completely comfortable, 3 is neutral, and 5 is very unpleasant.
5. Sensations associated with the emotion. Our emotions occur through our bodies, with the same chemical messengers often orchestrating the emotion with the bodily sensation. (See Candace Pert's *The Molecules of Emotions*, for more information about these connections, in the book list.)
6. Do you have thoughts or feelings in reaction to having the emotion in the first place? These are also called meta-feelings (as introduced in chapter 2) – meaning emotions or thoughts about your feelings (for expediency, we call this meta-feelings rather than meta-thoughts-and-feelings).

Chart 6B Emotion survey

Copy and add rows as needed

1 Emotion	2 Circumstances when you have it	3 How do you express it	4 Is it comfortable or unpleasant: 1-5 scale	5 Sensations	6 Reactions to it: Meta-feelings

Working with your survey

Our emotions can become distorted over time. Sometimes this is because we've felt pressures to emotionally lie to ourselves for any number of reasons. Other times, hiding or distorting our true emotions has been necessary to survive trauma or maltreatment, or has been rewarded. If such distortions of our emotional expression continued during our rapid postnatal brain development (also called 'childhood', see chapter 4), then these emotional distortions can remain long term. We likely won't recognise them, as we've felt these emotions in these ways, literally as long as we can remember (since our hippocampi wired themselves up!).

What we feel Vs what we do

We all need to find a balance between being honest with ourselves about how we feel, and what we do about those feelings. Obviously we can't always *express* each of our feelings. This would not necessarily serve us well and could possibly hurt our personal and/or professional relationships. But emotions we deny – don't allow ourselves to feel – are dangerous, leading to a number of health problems in body and mind.

Mismatched emotions – golden opportunities

Do you ever have emotional reactions that are out of proportion to the circumstances? Do you find that you can be surprised at how strongly you feel or react at times?

If you repeatedly experience certain emotions such as anger, hurt, feeling left out, or any others, that are disproportionate to the circumstances, this usually means it comes from early learning (see chapter 4), something that happened to you in your past. Usually this learning happened during the accelerated brain development of childhood and youth, having been woven in during development. How these triggers occur is discussed in more detail in chapter 9.

Mapping disproportionate emotions on to the past

Use chart 6C overleaf to record observations about these mismatches. This information will be used in a memory remodelling method (chapter 9) that helps take the power out of these reactions.

Columns 1 and 2 are self-explanatory.

For column 3, try to remember your earliest memories of feeling the same feeling that is being triggered out of proportion in the present. It's best to do this when you're having a disproportionate emotional reaction or shortly afterwards. Just think to yourself, 'Quick, when did I feel like this in the past?' Don't dwell on it – pick the first thing that comes to mind. If nothing comes to mind, leave it and try again next time.

There is no end to the possibilities, but here are some examples of present triggers and past learning that can sensitise us in the present to help explain this type of present-past connection.

Present trigger: Highly vulnerable to feeling left out, even when the function or gathering has little to do with you or you're not actually very interested.

Possible past learning-sensitisation: You may have moved many times as a child and as a result were often the new kid and were left out of things at the start of each new home location.

Present trigger: You feel mistreated and forgotten when others get praise or are rewarded for their efforts.

Possible past learning-sensitisation: You were doted on as a child, giving you an unrealistic idea of the amount of attention and accolades any one individual should expect as a healthy balance.

Present trigger: You feel immediately worried and frightened when someone is cross with you.

Possible past learning-sensitisation: You were mistreated during childhood or adult carers left the family abruptly without proper explanation or goodbyes.

Chart 6C Mismatched emotions

Make copies of this chart as useful.

1 Triggering circumstance	2 Disproportionate emotion	3 Earlier memories with same feeling

Save your column 3 responses for use in the memory remodelling method in chapter 9 that can gentle the effects of this past learning.

Masked emotions

Sometimes one emotion becomes larger and larger in our lives until it overtakes other feelings. This can happen when we feel or believe certain feelings are wrong or when we perceive social or other pressures not to feel certain emotions. Like all other habits of the mind, repetition strengthens this habit and we can come to no longer even feel the emotions we've masked long-term. The energy of the emotion will be diverted and often be experienced and/or expressed as another emotion or physical sensation or symptom. For example, in many societies women are frowned upon if they get angry, whereas nervousness or anxiety is more acceptable. For men, feeling overly kind or sympathetic can be frowned upon in many situations.

Emotion masking can also come from traumatic experiences when your safety and possibly even survival depended on you not expressing certain emotions. In these situations, our brains will help us survive by shrouding the emotions that are too difficult, awful or risky to experience. A 'risky' emotion could have been one that might make you do something that would put you or someone else in danger. For example, when we're children, we can't always afford to feel the normal anger towards someone who mistreats us because if we were to express it, we could risk enraging the abuser and engender further abuse towards us.

Any of us, constantly beset by one emotion, may be redirecting any number of different emotions into the one single type.

If we feel the real emotions rather than the the masquerading one(s), we will feel better for it in the long run. Experiencing our true feelings is necessary for good health of our minds and bodies. Feeling our real emotions will also improve our relationships with other people, and ourselves, and will help us see our true options more clearly.

Examples

Anger can mask hurt. Whereas anger tends to move and keep people away (leading to further hurt which will be expressed as masqueraded anger), letting others know you're hurt can bring people closer and inspire kindness.

Anxiety can mask many emotions including annoyance and anger. Sometimes people feel subconsciously it's more acceptable for them to be nervous. The nervousness could be used as a reason not to take a better, more challenging job. But the real reason may be that the person is concerned that doing so would impact their relationship with their partner. They believe the partner would not approve, which makes them angry at the partner (who hasn't expressed any opinion). But because feeling this anger would hurt the relationship, they don't express it. They feel anxious instead. Whereas genuine communication with the partner about these concerns could very well reveal that the partner is delighted with the decision to accept the position.

Emotion recognition exercise

If you find you feel any given emotion more than 40% of the time, ask yourself what other emotions might another person feel in those circumstances. Make a list of them and then ask yourself if you might feel them, every time you feel the over-felt emotion. Continue for a minimum of five days. It can take a while for the underlying feelings to come through, once they've been given 'permission'.

Numbness – warning sign

If you find that you feel emotionally numb, don't feel any of your usual emotions or such small versions of your usual emotions to be almost absent, you may be in the midst of a clinical situation that needs sorting. Emotional numbness can be a symptom of a concerning level of depression. It can also come from damping down high levels of distressing emotions for a long period. It also happens in grief. If this emotional numbness lasts for more than two weeks you are best advised to seek professional advice.

Summing Up

- Emotions are critical information for us, an essential part of rational thought. Without them, we'd be set adrift, unable to decide much of anything.
- A wide array of normal human emotions exists.
- Feeling our emotions is necessary for a healthy body and mind; forcing our feelings underground is related to numerous health problems.
- Our emotions come from a field of data about the outside world, our internal organs and bodies, along with our memories and past learning – synthesised in the brain. Increasing our ability to perceive our bodily functions can increase our emotional acuity.
- A number of emotional distortions can arise from social and personal pressures and our histories.
- Recognising and rebalancing these distortions increases our health and wellbeing.

Chapter Seven

Emotional Logic

Emotions follow their own logic; a set of natural and observable laws. Understanding them allows you to work with them. Many of the emotional problems we struggle with don't go away because we inadvertently work against these natural laws and this can even worsen the problems. Do you feel anxious too much of the time? Avoid certain situations or people in order to feel more comfortable? Do you feel compelled to do certain things repeatedly, although you don't really want to? Here you will learn techniques that work with the natural logic of emotions to rid yourself of these and other problems.

Natural laws of emotion

There are two natural characteristics of our emotions that are core to many anxiety-related problems. One is a law of learning, called avoidance learning, and the other is the natural pattern of emotional experience.

Avoidance learning

We all work to keep unwanted events from happening, but this can get overdeveloped in a false way that often gets out of hand. Let's say you do X in order to avoid Y. Many times this is perfectly reasonable, for example when you look both ways before crossing a street in order to avoid getting hit by a car. This works consistently. We have many experiences of avoiding cars by looking and this habit is duly strengthened in mind and brain.

But when the X is not really protecting you from the Y, and the Y never happens anyway so you never know it is unrelated to X, well then, you are accidentally learning a false connection. For example, let's say I have a fear of being attacked by goats and I believe that wearing red protects me. I wear red every day for 15 years and I have not been attacked by any goats even once during that time (never mind that I work in an office on the second floor), then my luggage is lost by the airline during a trip and I cannot find any red clothing to buy. Because me and my brain believe we've had 15 blissfully goat-free years because of my wearing red, I would find not wearing red horrendously frightening. After all, to me it seems I've had 100% success in fending off goats with my wardrobe, whereas I've had 0% experience *not* wearing red and seeing what happens.

Lack of natural testing

With avoidance learning, we don't spontaneously test it. We don't do X to avoid cataclysm Y, maintain a cataclysm-free life and then one day awaken to think, 'Hmmm, I think I'll *not* do X today and see if a cataclysm *does* happen, what fun!'. Because of this natural lack of testing, we end up only collecting ticks on the 'Do X, Avoid Y' side of our internal learning score sheet. (Remember, the brain processes our experience as a matter of proportion.) By purposefully collecting some ticks on the *other* side of our internal score sheets – 'Don't do X, Avoid Y' we start to even out the score. This releases us from the false learning and is the core to the most proven CBT techniques for anxiety-related problems as described overleaf (also see Edna Foa and John March's books in the book list).

Pattern of emotions

When you graph the intensity of emotions over time, you get a pattern: it increases, it peaks, and then it decreases.

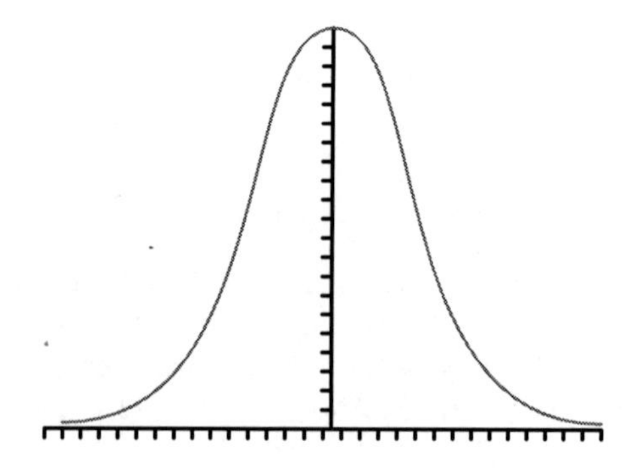

If we find an emotion uncomfortable, understandably we do things to give ourselves relief. But we may think we're having more impact than we are, because after a point, the emotion is going down anyway. This is essential in learning how to reduce anxiety, panic and obsessional problems. We (and our brains) mistakenly believe that our behaviours (done at the middle point, as shown in the diagram, for example) are reducing our discomfort. Many experiences of spuriously doing L to reduce M, then M goes down (all on its own) strengthen this belief. As with avoidance learning, it is paramount to collect ticks on the other side of the score sheet. As explained below, freeing ourselves from any number of problems, necessitates *not* doing our usual and waiting for the emotion to subside on its own. This teaches our brains this important lesson and releases us from needing to engage in our old ways.

Anxiety: What is it good for?

Anxiety is a part of our fear response. It includes all the same physiological changes and the emotional experiences of proper fear – just with*out* a tiger running after us, although it can feel just as frightening. Anxiety also stimulates the stress system which, when engaged long term, increases health risks and leads to changes in the brain (explained in more detail in chapter 8).

Feeling anxious is a normal part of life – when taking an exam, starting something new, performing, making a big decision and at other times. But we can also feel anxious too much of the time and in situations that don't warrant it. Anxiety can spiral out of control because anxiety in and of itself is frightening.

Anxiety problems

Specific fears

Some fears are the same the world over. Many of these fears, including snakes, heights and wariness of strangers, are also seen in most animals and have helped us survive, especially during our first 190,000 years on Earth. We are the only species that has gone from living in small groups of 30 or so, to living in metropolises of millions in a mere 10,000 years. Our genes have not changed dramatically in this small timescale. It may be that any of us who *don't* feel trepidation amongst throngs of strangers are the biologically odd ones.

Some of these universally common fears are listed below, with the clinical name in brackets.

- Crowds, crowded places, open places and fear of leaving a safe place (agoraphobia).
- Closed in places (claustrophobia).
- Heights (acrophobia) fear of flying can be included.
- New people and extreme shyness (social phobia).
- Performance – including non-professional performance such as speaking in front of groups (performance anxiety).
- Snakes (ophidiophobia).
- Spiders (arachnophobia).

Reducing fear and anxiety

Example 1: Fear of flying

Using the example below, make your own work plan.

- List all aspects of your fear. Break this down into smaller steps as in the example below. NB: Smaller is better. Unlearning the fear will be easier if you break it down into small bite-sized pieces and will increase your success with each smaller step, giving you overall better traction.
- Rate those steps as to how emotion-provoking they are (1 lowest-10 highest).
- Order them from least to most emotion-provoking.

Example 1: Fear of flying work plan

Order for working on	Situation	Anxiety Rating 1-10
1	Seeing an airline advertisement	1
2	Hearing people talk about flying somewhere	2
3	Seeing parked planes	4
4	Packing luggage	5
5	Handling airline tickets	6
6	Travelling to airport	7
7	Entering the airport	8
8	Flying with no turbulence and no seat belt required	8
9	Take-off	9
10	Turbulence or the 'seat belt' sign coming on	10
11	Landing	10

Fear of flying method

1. Practise the steady breathing method of your choice and mindfulness until you can do these readily and easily (instructions at the end of the chapter).
2. Start with the lowest rated step in your work plan.
3. Go through the first step while reducing your anxiety with the steady breathing (page 89).
4. On a scale of 1 (low) to 10 (highest), do not let your anxiety get any higher than 3 while engaging in each step. If your anxiety exceeds this level, continue with your breathing and introduce mindfulness until the anxiety subsides. This is important, because you don't want to accrue any more associative learning between what you fear and feeling frightened. This relearning allows you and your brain to collect experiences of the previously feared object or action that are not associated with fear.
5. Repeat the exercise at the first step, once or twice a day, daily, until you feel no more than a level 1 anxiety while doing it, two times in a row.
6. Repeat this process with each successive next step.

Example 2: Shyness, social phobia and agoraphobia work plan (Shyness-plus)

Fill out a work plan as explained for fear of flying. An example is below.

Example 2: Shyness-plus work plan

Order for working on	Situation	Anxiety Rating 1-10
1	Looking out the window at people passing by	1
2	Answering the phone when I know who it is	2
3	Speaking to a shop worker	4
4	Agreeing plans to socialise	5
5	Eating out	6
6	Leaving the house	7
7	Going to cinema or theatre	8
8	Answering the phone when I don't know who it is	8
9	Answering the door when I don't know who it is	9
10	Interacting with new people	9
11	Returning an item of shopping	10
12	Going to a busy shopping precinct	10
13	Going to a festival	10

Shyness-plus methods

These are similar to the methods for fear of flying, with a few differences in *italics*.

1. Practise the steady breathing method of your choice and mindfulness (pages 89 and 90) until you can do these readily and easily.
2. Start with the lowest rated step in your work plan.
3. Go through the first step while reducing your anxiety with the steady breathing.

4. On a scale of 1 (low) to 10 (highest), do not let your anxiety get any higher than 3 while engaging in each step. *Do not leave a situation in order to reduce your anxiety (see patterns of emotions page 80).* If your anxiety exceeds this level, continue with your breathing and introduce mindfulness until the anxiety subsides *before leaving the situation*.
5. Repeat the exercise at the first step, once or twice a day, daily, until you feel no more than a level 1 anxiety while doing it, for two times in a row.
6. Repeat this process with each successive next step.

Remember, all learning includes setbacks and some less successful days. Do not be daunted by this natural curve of learning. Continue with each step for a three-day minimum before deciding it's not working. If you remember learning any skill, driving, making a meringue, tiling a wall, you will remember mistakes and setbacks. But stick with it. Take heart. People previously unable to travel or leave their home have done so within weeks of starting such a programme.

Example 3: Obsessive-compulsive problems

Obsessive-compulsive disorder (OCD) problems include intrusive thoughts that are hard to resist. It often feels like doing an action (like washing hands, or checking a lock, for example) reduces the intrusive thought. But beware – this is a 'trick' of the OCD. The pressure to do the behaviour subsides, but not for long. **Remember the pattern of emotional expression** (page 80). Controlling OCD demands that you wait through the curve until the desire subsides by itself, so you don't mistakenly think it was the behaviour that did it. In fact, engaging in the behaviour tends to be 'moreish,' like scratching an itch that gets itchier.

OCD is likely biologically caused. It often feels like doing or thinking these things keeps people safe, or bad things from happening. You might feel compelled to think very disturbing thoughts, thoughts that you personally find upsetting. You might then spend considerable time trying to resist these thoughts or behaviours, usually unsuccessfully. OCD is like someone putting a nice big shiny button in front of you and being told 'whatever you do, don't touch it.' You can become completely absorbed with thinking about and resisting the OCD symptoms. Guilt and depression often accompany OCD.

The content of OCD is the same the world over, and includes: safety (checking light switches, appliances and the like); cleanliness (hand washing, cleaning and more); tidiness; symmetry; numbers, and others.

OCD is very successfully treated by a specialist type of CBT often combined with medication. Working through this book may not be sufficient. You can get professional help. Start by asking your GP for a referral. Other sources are listed in the help section at the back of the book.

Example 3: Obsessive-compulsive work plan

List all behaviour and thought OCD symptoms. Rate them as to how compelling they are from 1 (hardly compelling at all) to 10 (seemingly impossible to resist). A variety of symptoms are listed to illustrate the range of what can be part of OCD. All of these would not likely occur in one person.

Methods for OCD-like problems

1. Practise the steady breathing method of your choice and mindfulness until you can do these readily and easily (instructions at the end of the chapter).
2. Start with the lowest rated situation.
3. Don't take the urges and thoughts at face value. They are not truth, just 'brain hiccups'. The intrusive urges and thoughts are the OCD – not you.
4. Let the urge subside without giving in to it. This is critical!
   a. Use your breathing method while you let the urge subside (see pattern of emotions on page 80).
   b. Shift attention to anything else. You can use a very pleasant moment from chapter 5, or other distraction.
5. Repeat these steps every time the lowest ranked urge or thought intrudes, until you are able to swat it away like a gnat. And you will get to this point, if you continue with the practice.
6. Repeat the process with the next lowest rated urge and so forth.

CBT is highly successful for OCD. You can be freed of its grip and get back to your life. It can be hard work breaking the back of OCD. You need to keep on with the practice, even when you have hit a plateau. More success will come with your continued practice. For some people, maintenance CBT is necessary to keep it at bay. For more information on OCD, take a look at *Obsessive Compulsive Disorder – The Essential Guide*, Need2Know.

Order for working on	Situation	Anxiety Rating 1-10
1	Eating only odd numbers of things	1
2	Having to say a specific word to yourself when anyone mentions death	2
3	Needing to do things evenly on both sides of your body, for example if you scratch your left ear because it itches, you have to then scratch the right ear	3
4	Checking you've signed all letters the same number of times as the first number in the postcode of the recipient	5
5	Feeling compelled to say specific words and touching your nose, if anyone passes you while scratching their nose	6
6	Feeling like everything in your home must be perfectly symmetrical or someone you love will be in grave danger	7
7	Believing you will transmit dangerous germs to your loved ones from normal contact (even though you do not have any contagious diseases)	8
8	Washing your hands so often they bleed	8
9	Being compelled to think about things you find horrible, or disgusting, and then feeling awful about having thought them	9
10	Checking doors are locked in a certain order, and repeating the sequence seven times	9
11	Resisting sending rude emails that are not your usual style to your boss or other people in authority	10
12	Needing to tidy and clean the house perfectly because it feels like doing so keeps your family safe	10
13	Checking all appliances and electrical outlets, in a certain order, five times, before leaving the house	10

Panic attacks

These are sudden surges of high levels of fear that usually include acute physical changes including racing heart, palpitations, chest pain or discomfort, shortness of breath or difficulty breathing, profuse sweating, dizziness or fainting, nausea, numbness or tingling in your face, feet or hands, feelings of impending doom and more. Panic attacks are often mistaken for heart attacks. It is important to rule out a physical problem, if you've never had one before. Sometimes we know what causes the panic attack, but more often it's not clear. Being tired, worn out or stressed will increase the chances of one, if you're vulnerable to them.

Once you've had one, the fear of another can interfere with your functioning. It's important to remember the symptoms usually subside on their own in 10-20 minutes, as explained in the patterns of emotions section on page 80.

When people feel anxious or panicky, it is natural to want to leave the situation. In fact, the desire to escape is part of the fight, flight or freeze reaction. If you do leave the situation every time you feel panic or anxiety, you and your brain will think this is what relieved it. But the truth is that these feelings will go away naturally anyway. It's very important you stay in the place where you're feeling the anxiety and do the steady breathing and/or mindfulness at the very earliest warning signs, reducing – and eventually thwarting – the anxiety. The anxiety will dissipate and you will have one experience in your brain's log that leaving wasn't necessary. The more of these you collect, the less you will feel the need to escape, and the anxiety will start to leave you alone.

Relief from panic attacks

Breathe – Learn one of the breathing techniques below. This is critical, as slowing your breathing is proven to slow your heart. Slowing your heart will avert the escalating panic. Practise your breathing method daily (when you are not feeling anxious or panicked). Make this a daily habit, like brushing your teeth. This way you always have this skill ready, should you need it.

First signs – At the very first signs of rising panic, do your slowed breathing. *Do not leave*.

Not dangerous – Remember, despite the strong, horrendous feelings of panic – you are *not* in danger.

More information is in the help list.

Steady breathing

Deceivingly simple, but proven over the millennia, slowed breathing is an important technique to have in your 'tool bag', for life in general and for anxiety in particular. Breathing techniques for improving health date back to ancient meditation practices of 5,000 years ago. Slowing your breathing slows your heart rate, and stops the physiological aspects of anxiety. Simply *not* letting your heart rate increase is incredibly powerful in halting anxiety in its tracks; your adrenalin will not pump out, your stress hormones will not increase, and the feeling of fear will not come on.

Here are two proven breathing techniques. See which one you prefer.

Three-step breathing (or five, five and five)

- Breathe in *slowly* for a count of five.
- Hold your breath for a count of five.
- Exhale *slowly* for a count of five.
- Repeat the sequence a minimum of five times.

Four-step breathing (or square breathing)

- Breathe in *slowly* for a count of five.
- Hold your breath for a count of five.
- Exhale *slowly* for a count of five.
- Hold your breath for a count of five.
- Repeat the sequence a minimum of five times.

Practise before you need it

You will need to have a breathing technique at the ready for the previous work plans. Practise the breathing techniques when you are calm, at least once a day.

It is crucial that you breathe slowly and that you hold your breath when indicated in order for this to work. You can prove to yourself that steady breathing works. Take your pulse (see chapter 6 for instructions), do the breathing technique and take it again to see if your heart rate has decreased, even when you are not stressed to begin with.

'It is a commonly held view that meditation is a way to shut off the pressures of the world or of your own mind, but this is not an accurate impression. Meditation is neither shutting things out nor off. It is seeing clearly and deliberately positioning yourself differently in relationship to them.'

Jon Kabat-Zinn.

Mindfulness meditation

Mindfulness means being in the moment, being fully aware in the continual present without judgement or analysis. Mindfulness is a central part of Buddhist practice starting approximately 2,300 years ago. It was first introduced as part of Western talking therapies in Gestalt therapy in the 1940s (they called it 'Awareness'). Mindfulness is a core CBT method and numerous neuroscience studies demonstrate the brain basis.

We are often thinking about the past or the future and while doing so will miss our very lives as they occur. Because our memories record *wherever our minds are,* we could be on a beautiful beach, but if we can't stop thinking about past regrets or future worries, well then, this is what our brains will record. We'll miss the beach entirely. In this way, depressive, anxious and other non-adaptive thinking gets reinforced in our neural circuits. Even if our thoughts are not particularly troubling, but simply filled with meaningless details of daily life, we are still missing our very lives because our minds are elsewhere.

People who practise mindfulness have:

- Long-lasting stress reduction, both physical and psychological aspects.
- Reduced recurrence of depression or anxiety problems.
- Fewer problems with addiction.
- Greater happiness and wellbeing.
- Improved decision-making and related brain changes.

- Improved concentration and attention with related brain changes.
- Increased empathy.
- Expansion of the area of the brain used in regulating emotion, and better emotion regulation.
- Improved job performance, productivity and satisfaction.
- Improved circulatory health including increased blood flow, reduced blood pressure.
- Reduced risk and severity of heart disease, including reducing the risk of dying from it.

The mindful brain

When we are in an ordinary mood state (not depressed, anxious, stressed or otherwise perturbed) the left frontal cortex of our brain has *higher* activity than the right frontal cortex. (There are a number of naturally occurring asymmetries in our brain function. These may be different if you're left-handed.) In depression, this normal asymmetry disappears, with both sides being equal, or even reversed, with the right side having greater activity. Mindfulness meditation restores the normal asymmetry and can even enhance it. Studies using brain scans of Buddhist monks who are expert in this type of meditation found that they have unusually high left frontal lobe activity, compared to the right. One of the monks studied, Matthieu Ricard, who had the largest asymmetry, wrote a book on happiness (see the book list).

Mindfulness meditation: overview

Mindfulness is a practice, a way of bringing forth your inner subjective experience. The aim is to be completely in the current moment, aware of your bodily sensations and the world around you, but *not* to think about the past, the future or actually *anything.* Overleaf are some methods that help. It can be helpful to listen to a CD, DVD or webcast where someone gives instructions while you do this. See the book and help lists for resources.

- Get in a comfortable position, sitting or lying down.
- You may close your eyes, but it's not necessary.
- Pay attention to your breathing, concentrating on nothing but your breathing (don't count, this is different than the breathing methods previously discussed). Observe your breathing in, and out . . . in and out . . . in and out, and nothing else.
- Quiet your mind. As thoughts come through your mind, release them. Observe them but *don't* 'take them down' and continue thinking about them. Treat them like clouds floating by. Observe, and release all thoughts as you continue to concentrate on your breathing.
- Do not judge or analyse your thoughts. Remember – thoughts are just thoughts. We have millions of them, but just because we have them, does not mean they are true, meaningful, or valuable.
- Do a 'body inventory'. This is another method of inducing mindfulness. You start with either your head or your feet and consciously be aware of how that part of your body feels, then consciously let that part of your body go completely relaxed. Continue, methodically, up or down your body until you've reached the other end.
- Experience your senses. Become fully aware of what you see, hear, smell, taste, and feel on the external parts of your body such as temperature, any breezes and more.

Mindfulness reminders

Mindfulness is not meant to be restricted to formal meditative practices, but something that is incorporated into our lives. After you've started to learn mindfulness meditation, choose things in your usual environment to serve as prompts for you to practise mindfulness right then and there, if even for a few minutes. A building you pass daily, a stop sign at the end of your road – anything can serve as a prompt to practise, fully inhabiting each moment of your life.

Summing Up

- Emotions do have their own logic, and understanding this logic empowers you to be free of a number of problems.
- Avoidance learning is when we inadvertently think our actions are keeping an unwanted outcome at bay, when in reality they aren't.
- It is important to let yourself collect other experiences that let you provide balance.
- Strong emotions, including anxiety and the urges that come with OCD subside naturally, even if we don't do anything. This is key to letting our brains learn that we don't have to give in to false urges and beliefs, but can let them pass without engaging them.

Chapter Eight

Your Choice – Your Life

Do you feel stressed a lot of the time? Feel like you never get to do the things you want to do? Do you often worry about what other people think? Do you have problems saying 'no'?

This chapter looks at stress, the large and the small – what we can control and what we can't – and how stress affects us and what we can do about it.

At times in most of our lives, pushing ourselves beyond our usual capacity is appropriate, the right thing to do. Life includes real problems, hardships, loss and tragedies, as well as other more ordinary stresses that require us to act beyond the call of duty. There may be times we *want to* work extra hard on a project or opportunity close to our hearts. But we also need a balance. If we 'run on fumes' for months or even years, this will take its toll on our mental and physical health; this is also a way to induce clinical depression.

'In the UK, nearly one-half a million people report suffering from work-related stress, depression or anxiety in 2007-8. This has doubled since the early 1990s.'

Health and Safety Executive, UK Government.

There is no such thing as '120%' effort

Many jobs demand long hours and ask you to increase your effort and productivity every year. After a while it becomes nonsensical. Our interpersonal reserves are *not* infinite. It is possible to exhaust our psychological resources – the mind is real (despite Descartes' error, chapter 1).

The stress axis – mind and body

When we're faced with imminent danger we go into 'flight, fight or freeze' mode. ('Freeze' has been added to the list recently; sometimes doing nothing, becoming seemingly paralysed, is our best option when faced with a serious danger.)

This is also called the stress axis. It developed for short deployment. This axis includes parts of the brain and body that orchestrate various emergency responses to danger. Blood is shunted away from the organs to the limbs for faster running. We naturally want to empty our bowels and bladder – the more likely to outrun our pursuer. This is why we can get a wobbly stomach when we are stressed or nervous or fearful.

This survival system has served us well over our 200,000 year life as the species Homo sapiens. For most of this time, we've lived in small bands, roaming around following natural food sources. During the majority of the first 190,000 years as a species, the dangers we faced meant either we *were* lunch or we made it home for lunch. Then about 10,000 years ago we discovered agriculture – growing our own food, allowing us to stay put. With more recent changes brought on by the industrial revolution, we rarely have to run from a tiger or fight off an intruder.

Today, this emergency survival system often gets deployed by work and life stressors and can stay raised for days or even years. Many biological changes caused by stress and chronic deployment of the stress cascade (increased adrenalin, cortisol, and many other changes) literally wear out our bodies *and* our brains.

Stress increases health risks

The stress axis has many effects on brain and body. Within 20 minutes of increased stress, the capacity of our immune system that fights off disease, is reduced. Research shows that chronic stress increases our chances of incurring numerous health problems. Some examples are listed below.

- Heart disease.
- Cancers.
- Digestive disorders.
- Diabetes (Type II).
- Depression.
- Anxiety disorders.

Chronic stress reduces the size of the hippocampus – the same part of the brain that becomes larger in London taxicab drivers as they learn all the London streets – 'doing the Knowledge'. Post-traumatic stress can also reduce the size of the hippocampus. Robert Sapolsky is one of the seminal researchers in the field of stress and how it works in the brain and body as explained in his excellent book *Why Zebras Don't Get Ulcers: An Updated Guide to Stress* (see the book list).

Yet the brain remains flexible. Hippocampi recover, as can we, from stresses large and small. In the following pages you are shown how to recognise stress, how to curtail it and how to reduce its impact in future.

Listen to yourself – Stress survey

Feeling stressed, like other emotions, is information; a 'message to yourself from yourself'. It is a signal that you are operating in a deficit mode and need to replenish and recharge. Listen to this signal and do something about it.

Overleaf are many of the more common signs of stress. Indicate if you have each one, and if so, for how long.

If you have one or more signs from each of the four categories overleaf (sleep, emotional, cognitive and physical) for two weeks or longer, you are experiencing an unhealthy level of stress. Overleaf are step-by-step methods to reduce it now and in the future.

Chart 8A - Stress Survey

Sign of stress	Do you have it?	For how long?
1. Sleep signs		
Difficulty sleeping.		
Sleeping too much.		
2. Emotional signs		
Irritability.		
Resentment.		
Wanting to leave the situation – escape.		
3. Cognitive signs		
Reduced concentration.		
Increased mistakes.		
Short-term memory problems.		
4. Physical signs		
Digestive system problems.		
Headaches.		
Muscle and body aches.		
Increased sweating.		

Control and stress: learned helplessness

Remaining proactive in dealing with stress, as well as our outlook on it, are key to reducing its impact. This was revealed in the 'learned helplessness' studies started in 1967 by Dr Martin Seligman (one of the early cognitive behavioural therapy researchers) and colleagues. These studies tested dogs in pairs. They found that dogs who received random low level foot shocks, but had a lever to stop it, did not suffer with stress or other problems. In comparison, dogs receiving the exact same duration and level of shock, but who had no control over it (it stopped when the other dog pressed the lever) suffered considerably. Strikingly, when the dogs with no control over the shock were later put in a situation where they could escape it by simply jumping over a short wall, they didn't even try. They laid down and whimpered, having learned from their past experience that the shock was inescapable; they had 'learned to be helpless'. In comparison, the dogs who had been able to turn off the shock, readily jumped over the walls when presented with that situation.

The dogs who had learned helplessness, developed a canine version of depression – disturbed sleep, poor relationships with other dogs and people, poor eating and they no longer groomed themselves.

However, not all the dogs gave up in the face of uncontrollable stress. Approximately one-third of these dogs actively and successfully worked to avoid subsequent shock – they did not act as though all stress was unavoidable.

Subsequent studies with humans have identified traits that protect against learned helplessness: optimism; not taking the stress personally; realising and believing that not everything is stressful, and not all the time.

Learned helplessness is an important model of how depression can develop. Further experiments using this paradigm with rats found that those receiving shocks with no levers to turn it off were more likely to get cancer if injected with a cancer-causing virus than their lever-pressing counterparts. Dr Seligman has gone on to study how to increase happiness, not just reduce depression (see the book list). These methods are being taught in 60 UK schools to teach young people CBT methods.

Harnessing stress

So how do you balance being proactive in dealing with stress without becoming a control freak? It helps to recognise that we can't control many things in life and it's not healthy – even possible – to try to control everything. But we can control how we live with, and through the stresses in our own lives. In fact, a wealth of research shows that sometimes, we come through stress more finely honed versions of ourselves. Like gold through fire, development is driven by struggle and mastery.

The 'why me?' warning

If you find yourself asking 'why me?' this is a sign you are taking life too personally. Things happen across the world, to millions of people all the time, including sad and tragic things. Many events are part of nature; it's truly nothing personal.

Take stock

- Some methods are useful for stressors of all durations. Other methods are more pertinent for specific types of stresses. These types are not mutually exclusive.
- Long term: Will this be a long-term effort on your part, such as caring for a seriously ill loved one or accommodating to long-term physical changes in yourself?
- Medium term: These include challenges such as finding a new job, ending an unhealthy relationship, changing aspects of your living situation that induce stress, such as too much isolation.
- Daily stressors: It can be hard to say 'no' to seemingly small extra requests or demands, but a steady diet of saying 'yes' can lead to an unbalanced, stressful, and unhealthy situation. See superhero syndrome on page 102.

Long term: tragedy and trauma

Unwanted and unexpected events can change our lives and our options, options we previously had taken for granted. Below is a general approach to such life-changing events that you can modify and apply as is useful.

Grief period

Whether you've lost some physical abilities due to an injury; an important relationship ends; a loved one dies; or other major unwanted event occurs; you need to give yourself a proper period to grieve for the loss. Loss happens in many forms, not just death. Research shows that it can be up to two years for grief over the death of a loved one to be mostly resolved. This time period varies. Allow yourself two to six months, depending on the depth of the loss, to heal through the initial stages of shock and grief. Disbelief, anger, resentment, sleep disturbance, energy loss, changes in appetite, as well as deep sadness are all normal aspects of grief (see the help and book lists for more resources).

Be kind to yourself – reduce demands in your work and personal life; recognise your increased need for rest and possibly sleep; do more of what you like. (Do pleasurable things that are legal and safe – do more of them!)

Warning:

If you find yourself having thoughts of suicide, especially if you start to plan how you might carry it out, seek help immediately. You can call the Samaritans for immediate help (see the help list). See your GP for a referral to the appropriate service. Of course, if you have taken too many tablets or injured yourself in other ways that may be life-threatening, call emergency services or get to accident and emergency to be examined.

As you start to recover from the initial stages of the grief and feel you want to do more, start to think and plan. What options do you have? If this were happening to someone else, what would you think they should do? The approaches described under Life's Challenges and Superhero Syndrome can help at this stage.

Medium term – life's challenges

We often feel like we don't have a choice but to remain in stressful or otherwise inadequate work and interpersonal situations. Learning from the dogs in the learned helplessness experiments described previously, you need to rethink your options and become active in working towards your better future.

Re-prioritise

We can often feel stuck in situations. This can be because we're not used to considering new ideas, because we find change difficult or because we've bought into a value system, often without realising it. If you are staying in an empty relationship or a job you hate because of finances, consider this: numerous studies show that beyond being able to provide our necessities –

shelter, food or health care – added wealth does *not* significantly increase happiness. Happiness comes from feeling connected to others and productive activities, whether a loved hobby, a rewarding job, or both.

If you feel trapped in a job, location, relationship or other situation, explore your options and start planning. If you feel trapped in a job for example, merely looking at the job listings at least once a week (preferably *not* at your desk at work) will bring relief. There are always options.

Beware the 'yes, buts'

When people suggest ways out of your predicament, do you find yourself saying or thinking, 'yes, but . . . '? If you respond to all ideas and ways forward with 'yes, but', then something else is holding you back from making the changes you want.

- Are there some positive aspects to your current situation that keep you there?
- Do you find change difficult or uncomfortable? Break down the change process into smaller steps and let yourself get used to the change bit by bit. If you get anxious or uncomfortable just thinking about the change, practise imagining yourself in the new situation while also practising feeling relaxed. Mentally rehearse realistic but calm experiences in your changed life.
- If it were someone else in your circumstances, what advice would you give them?

Superhero syndrome – when you can't say no

Do you have problems saying 'no' to any and all requests that come your way? For many of us, this snowballs out of control even becoming a long-term lifestyle. Many people find they've neglected their own lives after years of putting everyone first.

This style of interacting with others is also called 'co-dependence' or 'pathological altruism'; taking on other's needs, wants and even their lives, as though they are ours. This is only appropriate when you are raising a child and, even then, it needs to be balanced for the child's health as well as yours.

Signs of superhero syndrome

- You rarely say 'no' or can't say 'no' when requested to help.
- You make decisions based on what you think other people want.
- You prefer to do things yourself, otherwise (you believe) they won't be done properly.
- You find yourself regularly thinking about other people's problems and how to fix them.
- You feel unappreciated a lot of the time.
- You pride yourself in being the one person everybody turns to.
- You become impassioned about other people's interests at the expense of your own.

How did I get here?

On the face of it, it can seem like you're being a good person, always helping, going the extra mile. Of course it's important to care about our fellow humans, but, once again, it's a matter of balance.

Some of us were overly involved in a caretaking role as children, priming us to feel comfortable in this role as an adult. This does not necessarily mean you were physically taking care of the household or adults when you were a child, although you may have been. If your relationships with adults during your childhood included putting your personal or even educational needs aside to please or appease the adult(s), and this happened for prolonged periods, then this can also set you up for co-dependence, or superhero syndrome as an adult.

Take off your cape

When helping isn't so helpful

It's important to understand that although it may seem like it's helpful to others to do so much for them, it isn't. It isn't good for you, because you end up living other people's lives, not your own. It isn't good for the other person either because they will not learn how to do things for themselves. They can feel helpless and incompetent if they are never allowed to do things for themselves and they may start to resent you.

You are wrong more than you know

Basing your behaviour on what you surmise other people want is a dangerous game. You will often be wrong. In this way, you can end up doing things you don't really want to do, but believe are to please other people, when you are not even pleasing them.

Feel the guilt and *don't* do it anyway

Below are step-by-step methods for breaking the codependent, superhero behaviour. Start by filling in chart 7A as each column for entries is explained below.

The behaviour – Examples are given. Yours may differ.

- **Can't say 'no'** – These include not being able to say 'no' to doing extra work at your job; to children and other loved ones, including minor favours such as lifts, making tea and so on; to friends' requests; to strangers who ask to go in front of you in queue, for example.
- **What others want** – When you act on what you assume others want, without asking. We can make decisions large and small – from what to have for dinner, to which house we buy or holiday we take – based on what we think others want. Don't assume you know. Ask, and ask directly. It often happens that two people act on what they believe the other person wants, when the truth is that both wanted the same, but another option.

- **Done properly** – When you do things yourself because you feel others don't do them properly. This can include household chores, when you need to work with others, tasks at work, or events with friends. Are you the one who always organises nights out?

Circumstances

Who does this happen with? Make a separate entry for behaviours that happen regularly, but with different people. For example, if you have difficulty saying 'no' to your colleague when they ask for a lift home even when it's inconvenient for you and you also have trouble saying 'no' to your teenager every time they want a lift, then enter each one separately, as it is likely harder to say 'no' to some people in your life than others. This will come into play when you start your habit stopping method.

Habit strength

How much does each situation tug at you – how hard is it to resist being the superhero in each circumstance? Rate each habit from 1 (very weak) to 10 (very strong; most difficult to break).

Chart 8B – Stopping superhero syndrome

Make copies of the chart below as useful.

1 The behaviour	2 Circumstances: Who, what, when, where	3 Habit strength: 1 (weakest) –10 (strongest)

Stopping superhero syndrome

You start with the lowest strength-rated habit and work your way up. If more than one has the same score, it doesn't matter what order you do them in. Below are general methods for you to adopt to your specific needs.

- **Prepare** a general declination statement to have at the ready. It can be hardest to say 'no' when we're caught off guard, when people surprise you with their requests. People don't say, 'Okay, I'm about to ask you something you really don't want to do, but feel obliged to, so get ready.' They just ask. To prepare for this element of surprise, develop a general statement you can use *and practise it,* aloud is best. It is easier to say something when you've said it and heard it out loud before. Something like, 'I'd love to help you, but let me check my diary' works. This communicates your good intentions (many of us are worried about other's perceptions of us should we say 'no'), and also gives you time to think if you really want and are able to oblige in this instance.

- **The right to change your mind**. Old habits take a while to retrain and you will probably still accidentally say 'yes' sometimes when you don't want to. Especially as you start this learning. It is perfectly okay to change your mind. You can always explain that you had momentarily forgotten about a previous engagement. *Remember, you are not the only way the other person can get this need met.* If you don't give someone a lift to the shops, they may end up meeting an old (or making a new) friend on the bus. It is not your responsibility to make everyone's lives easier and if they learn for themselves they'll be empowering themselves.

- **Withstand the guilt** and other difficult feelings stimulated by *not* engaging in your usual behaviour. *Remember, these feelings will pass* whether you jump to the rescue or not. If you give in to your old behaviour, your poor brain will accidentally think the feelings passed *because* you gave in to doing the behaviour. And your brain needs the experience of the feelings going away *without* you doing the behaviour to learn this new association.

- **Good enough *is* good enough**. If you have problems letting other people help and feel you have to do everything yourself in order for things to be done to your standards, you will need to withstand the feeling that the job is not being done properly in the interest of friendship. This is particularly difficult if you have perfectionist tendencies. But you can really hurt relationships over time by being continually demanding and perfectionist. When you have the urge to insist someone uses a different plate than the one they already have out, or to grumble and redo someone's effort to help, remember that by doing so you are likely to hurt their feelings, or at the very least, annoy them. And your annoyance can feel personal to the other person, and over time, such repeated interchanges will puts dings in this relationship.

- **Hold steady** and continue practising your new ways. All learning happens on a curve. You will get better at it and it will become easier over time.
- As you eradicate each unwanted behaviour, tackle the next one up the rating scale. Revise your methods in response to what works for you.

Summing Up

- Stress increases when our survival system engages – the flight, fight or freeze response to immediate danger.
- In the long term, stressful jobs and personal life crises raise the stress axis in our bodies and brain. Long-term engagement of the stress system increases a number of physical diseases – heart and digestive problems among others – and has a negative impact on our brain tissue.
- Attitude is central to reducing stress.
- We can teach ourselves to be more proactive in situations where we feel helpless.
- It's important we realise that unpleasant and terrible events are an integral part of life and that they are not personal statements the universe directs just at us.
- Exploring options, making plans and acting on those plans are important means of reducing stressful situations we cannot immediately change such as jobs.
- We can use well-founded methods to rid ourselves of the unhealthy habit of never saying 'no' and of the burdensome feeling we have to do everything ourselves and perfectly. In so doing, we shed the daily stresses that, if continued over years, can rob us of precious life experience.

Chapter Nine

Taming Triggers

Have you ever said or done something before you realised you said or did it? Do you ever have emotions or thoughts that jolt through you, but don't fit the situation? In this chapter we examine those triggers that move us to feelings and actions and discuss how to shift these experiences in more positive directions.

'Remember not only to say the right thing in the right place, but far more difficult still, to leave unsaid the wrong thing at the tempting moment.'

Benjamin Franklin.

When we've been triggered into saying harsh things or even lashing out physically, we can be left feeling guilty, embarrassed and ashamed, not to mention confused about what happened.

Other times people find themselves acting heroically before they 'know what they're doing'. A man walking home from work, once found himself diving over a bridge railing into the river without knowing why. Then, he realised he'd heard the desperate cries of a mother whose young child had fallen in. Luckily he had once been a competitively-trained diver and he saved the child.

The brain's short cut

There's a brain explanation for these quick reactions which seem to happen outside of our awareness. They do. Our brains process information in a step-wise manner, from raw data (e.g. the colour 'blue'), to multi-sensory data (someone wearing a blue coat), to processing through memory (that's my mate in that old blue coat), to evaluating any danger and appropriate reaction (I like him, I'll wave). It works this way for all the senses. The length of the neural circuits involved and the conduction speeds are known; how long such processing takes can be reliably predicted – in milliseconds.

It was quite a surprise when Dr Joseph E LeDoux, now one of the world's top experts in the neuroscience of emotion, came across another pathway, a short cut for emotional information. He discovered a direct route from the sensory processing to the amygdala, a part of the brain that underpins fear, rage and emotional learning (also discussed in chapters 4 and 7). The direct route, from sensation to amygdala is shorter and quicker, because it bypasses the cortex, the conscious part of the brain. Hence, our brains are wired to make quick decisions about danger before we have a chance to think about it. This makes sense from an evolutionary point of view. Those of us who have this short cut (most animals do) are more likely to survive any number of life and death circumstances compared to those individuals who might stand around and consider all the possibilities.

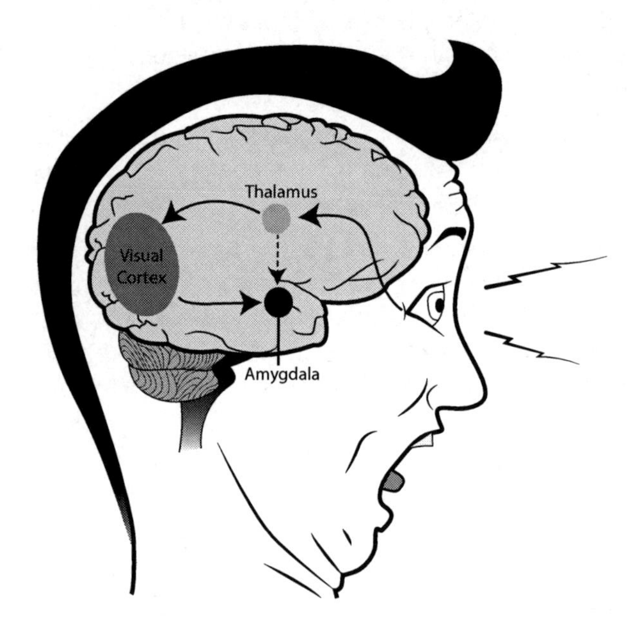

The LeDoux short cut is the dotted arrow from thalamus to amygdala, bypassing the longer route to through the visual cortex.

Emotional priming

Prior potent and early emotional learning will prime our amygdalae to recognise what is highly dangerous (see chapter 4). This is not limited to physical danger, but includes events related to high levels of negative emotions. For example, if you suffered bullying, humiliation or other forms of maltreatment by someone who always used a particular phrase, or wore a particular piece of clothing, then hearing that phrase or seeing similar clothing, could trigger the associated emotion – in this case humiliation or fear. Your amygdala sends immediate orders to react – to protect you. This all happens before your poor old cortex has a chance to catch up with the situation and you're stuck, wondering why you're feeling as you are and why you just did whatever it was you did when 'nothing's happened'. You're unaware of the trigger because your cortex hasn't yet caught up. You also may not remember the content of the memory – the who, what, when, where – because content memories are not as long-lasting as the emotional part as discussed in chapter 4.

Anger, fear, hurt, withdrawal and feelings of being emotionally paralysed are the most common reactions to triggers that trouble us. You may find you are more aware of any trigger-reaction sequences now that you've read about them. The methods that follow can defuse their power.

Chart 8A – Trigger map

Entries for each column are explained. Examples are given, but your experiences may be different than those illustrated here. There are no 'right' answers, of course.

Box 1 – Triggers

- People as triggers. Triggers can be someone acting in a certain way. Very angry people can be triggers, as can very meek people, as can any other type of behaviour. Sometimes certain types of people, such as those in authority, those in a position of service, can also be triggering, as can people in specific roles, or professions.

- Situations as triggers. Making a mistake or being caught in one, being disappointed or letting others down, being asked to take on responsibilities we don't want, or being denied an opportunity we long for are a few examples.
- Sensations as triggers. Music, other sounds, pictures, faces, aromas and other sensations can be triggers. Sometimes this starts suddenly, where the item or experience had *not* brought back any memories before, or at least not for a long time.

Box 2 – What you do

What do you say or do when you're triggered? Do you lash out verbally? Seek reassurance? Strike out physically towards objects or people? Storm off? Slam doors? Get angry inside, but can't express it? Isolate yourself? Become paralysed, unable to act?

Box 3 – What you think

What are your thoughts during these trigger-sequence events? That you're worthless? Unlovable? Undeserving? Not a good person? That you'll never be able to change or get control over being triggered? That other people are no good? That others will never understand or appreciate you? That you'll never fit in?

Box 4 – What you feel

Anger is commonly triggered via the amygdalae short cut. The anger can be so intense that the person has trouble *not* acting on it and may have problems with violence. Intense feelings of wanting to be aggressive against others can be triggered in this way. Other common feelings include fear, anxiety, trepidation, helplessness, hopelessness or feeling trapped. Pleasant and joyful feelings can also be triggered.

Box 5 – Felt like this before?

What is your earliest memory of *feeling* like this before. Triggers are usually an indication that you have had some prior emotional learning that developed these connections in your amygdala. That's why they can be triggered now. Once you've identified the likely early learning that set up this trigger, remember that this is what is really driving this trigger-reaction sequence, and not the current situation. The content of any early memories of feeling this way may not be available to you, as summarised below.

Chart 9A – Trigger map

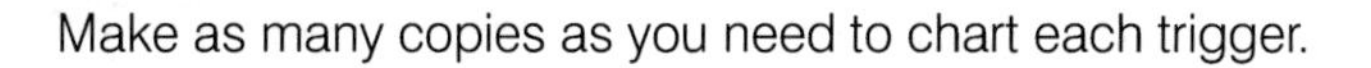

Make as many copies as you need to chart each trigger.

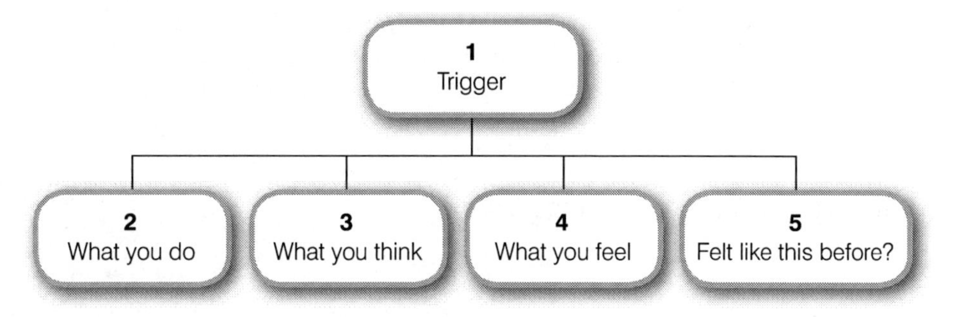

The amygdala never forgets

As explained above, we often don't have access to the content of the memories that evoked the triggered response for one of two reasons:

1. The intensity of the initial emotional learning was such that your brain decided it was important to activate this quick warning system – the LeDoux short cut described previously – to make sure you recognise this situation if it comes up again and are able to protect yourself.
2. The emotional parts of memories are longer lasting. The content may have faded for a number of reasons. In the case of prior mistreatment, sometimes our brains make things fade to protect us, but the emotional parts of the learning tend to linger.

Taming triggers – retraining your amygdala

Identify trigger warnings. Using the trigger warning map, see if you can identify any warnings.

- Warnings:

  Certain situations?

  Specific people?

  Types of places?

  Objects?

  Sensations – sounds, sights, smells?

- Early warnings – Can you anticipate when you might be faced with a trigger? For example if you had been traumatised in a school office, schools or similar buildings or offices may trigger you. In this way you could anticipate when you would be travelling near such a place. A vast array of things can be triggers.

Chart 9B Trigger warning map

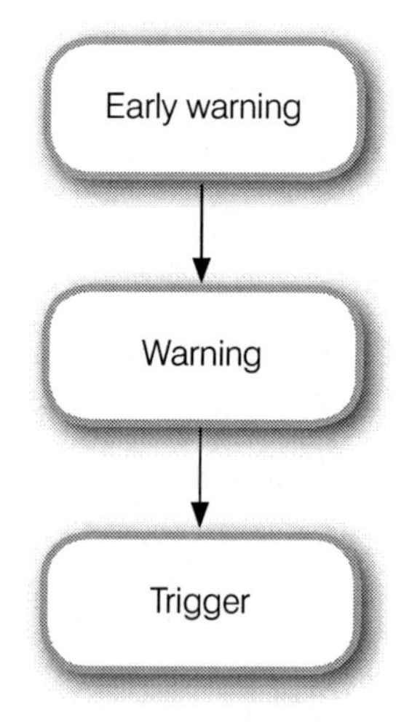

Taming triggers – method

Anticipate triggers. When you know or even just think a trigger is coming, be kind to yourself and:

Nip it in the bud. It is always easiest to stop a behavioural-emotional sequence at the earliest stage possible. Doing the techniques at the early warning stage is best.

Breathe. Using the techniques in chapter 7. To slow heart rate and lower the other physical aspects of the stress axis that is about to get stimulated.

Blast from the past. Remember that the trigger is just the touch paper to the prior emotional learning – it's not really about what's happening now.

Mantra Ready. Decide on a phrase to repeat to yourself as you anticipate or are in a triggering event, such as 'This feeling is coming from the past it's okay now', 'This is the *not* the past', or 'Quiet, you old amygdala – the real trouble's over!'. Any such statement will help your brain learn the difference between the past and present.

Stay in the present. What is really happening in the present? Use the breathing technique you chose (chapter 7) to reduce your level of emotional arousal and focus on the real situation in front of you.

Avoid avoidance

If you are highly distraught when around triggering situations, then you may be best advised to avoid them *in the short term.* You do not want to use avoidance in the long term because it will make your brain think you do need to avoid such situations to remain safe, as explained in chapter 7. Instead, you want to expose yourself to triggering situations in a gentle and graded manner as described in chapter 7.

NB: If you have problems with violence or aggression being triggered then it is important you remove yourself from the triggering situation. Use the memory revising techniques overleaf until the emotions that are elicited by such triggering events are reduced and until you feel well able to control any violent urges. It's advisable to get some professional input to reduce the problem more quickly and to keep it from escalating over time.

Memory remodelling

This technique is excellent for painful memories that bother you and difficult memories that may come back as you work to tame your triggers. This method has been used over the centuries and has been described in texts from different cultures. Neuroscience offers an explanation for this otherwise far-fetched sounding method. Two aspects of the brain basis of memory explain how it works. First, as explained above, the content and the emotions of a memory are stored separately.

Second, memories are not static, but modified, even if only slightly, with every retrieval, before being re-saved. This is similar to opening a computer document and making a few changes before re-saving it.

Method overview

1. Choose your target memory: intrusive, unpleasant or upsetting memories; or memories related to your triggers.
2. Imagine a *satisfying* resolution to the scenario in the memory you choose. The ending you choose does not have to be realistic, or even possible. It just has to be something you could get immersed in imagining. For example, let's say someone had a painful memory of someone being very disappointed with them, and then leaving. You could imagine standing up for yourself in a way you could not at the time. You could imagine the person stopping midstream and apologising. You could imagine the person as a helium balloon that floats away as they and their harsh words get progressively fainter until you can no longer see or hear them.
3. Practise the imagined satisfying resolution a few times.
4. Pick a reminder within the 'scene' of the unpleasant memory; a physical aspect of the 'scene', a piece of furniture, a post box, someone arriving, a sound or any other feature of your choosing.
5. When the unpleasant memory recurs (if you haven't already started), notice your chosen reminder to help prompt you to substitute the imagined satisfying resolution (number 2 above).

6. Insert the satisfying resolution each time the memory recurs.
7. Repeat until the memory no longer bothers you

No one is suggesting that the memory will disappear or that we will eventually convince ourselves it happened differently. Nor would we necessarily want to alter such memories. What this technique does is reduce the emotional intensity associated with the memory, which in turn makes it less 'memorable', which in turn makes it come to mind less often. Eventually it will completely stop rising up spontaneously.

Repeat the memory rewriting technique with each upsetting memory you'd like to diminish. It is best to work on one memory at a time.

Lucid dreaming

Are you haunted by recurring nightmares or bad dreams? Although it may sound far-fetched, you can remodel your dreams using a similar technique called 'lucid dreaming'. This technique was first described in the 5th century by St. Augustine of Hippo and by Tibetan buddhists practising a form of yoga starting in the 8th century. A surge of recent studies in Europe, Israel and the US are finding numerous benefits to our waking lives from lucid dreaming. These include improved decision making, lower levels of mental health problems, better ability to deal with new trauma, and better sports performance. This all may be related to strengthening part of the brain involved in decision-making and more.

'Many people who learn lucid dreaming find they are better able to manage uncomfortable emotional experiences during wakefulness as a "side effect!"'

In lucid dreaming you learn to be aware that you are dreaming *while you are dreaming.* You then manipulate the dream to make it non-traumatic.

This is an evidence-based method that's particularly helpful in reducing trauma-related recurrent nightmares. The method below is a modified form of Dr LaBerge's MILD (Mnemonic induction of lucid dreams) technique.

Lucid dreaming method

1. Don't worry. It won't get worse. It is a common concern that if you actively manipulate your nightmares, they will be even worse, but this is not true. The more you take control, the quicker they are no longer frightening.

2. Look for dream markers. While awake, remember the dream. Find something in the nightmare that tells you it's a dream and not real. Pick a dream marker that is *not* emotionally laden, such as something in the surroundings (furnishings you know are not like they are in real life, for example).

   Practise visualising this aspect of the scenery while saying to yourself, 'I see 'X' which means I am dreaming'. Practise this a few times a day.

3. Dream remodelling opportunities. What could happen differently that would remove the frightening aspects of the nightmare? Could some other people come in and stop the events from unfolding? Could the assailant be rendered powerless?
4. Instruct lucid dreaming. Place pen/pencil and paper next to your bed. Before going to sleep each night instruct yourself to be aware while dreaming. Pick a specific sentence to say a few times each night before going to sleep, something like, 'I will be aware that I'm dreaming when I'm dreaming and I am in charge of the dream!'
5. Write down any dreams you remember upon awakening, whenever that is.
6. If you awaken in the middle of the night, repeat the lucid dreaming instruction.
7. Once dreaming look for the dream markers. This will let you know you are dreaming.
8. If a nightmare starts – insert the remodelled version.
9. Note progress upon awakening.

Please 'suspend disbelief' and continue with the lucid dreaming practice for a minimum of 10-14 days. It really does work! Lucid dreaming takes practice and even very able lucid dreamers will not be successful every night. With consistent use, the frequency and intensity of the nightmares will decrease and in many instances stop.

Summing Up

- Many of us have had the experience of saying or doing something 'before we know what we are doing'.
- A recently discovered short cut between parts of our brain explains how certain things can trigger strong emotions, often disproportionate to the situation; we can diffuse these triggers and heal from prior events that caused them.
- Step-by-step instructions for techniques to remodel painful, haunting memories exist.
- It is even possible to drive your dreams and deflate the power of nightmares. Lucid dreaming is an ancient, and currently scientifically studied, technique that lets you do just that. In these ways you can use your neuroanatomy to diminish the power your past holds over your present and future.

Chapter Ten

Maintaining and Boosting Gains

CBT is a set of skills useful across our lives, a methodology for our minds. It is a set of universally useful and flexible tools for living life as it happens. CBT reduces recurrence of depression, anxiety and stress and lowers our vulnerability to addiction. Just as other healthy habits need to be maintained, so do your newly-honed CBT skills. This chapter examines methods to maintain your gains, explains how CBT fits into overall health and offers ways to define and consider your long-term life goals.

Taking stock

Using the chart below, list each problem you've been working on and what percentage of work remains (0% means it's all gone). Write the type of CBT maintenance you will apply (you may get ideas from the section overleaf). Add rows as needed.

Chart 10A Taking stock

Problem	Percentage remaining	CBT maintenance

Pulling weeds

CBT will completely and permanently abolish some habits. It is also natural for old habits to crop up occasionally. This is *not* a sign of failure. For many of us, the old unwanted habits existed for a long time, even decades; hence the neural circuitry is well established and will be quite robust! This happens to everyone, regardless of the type of learning. Ever try driving on the other side of the road? Or speaking another language? If you have, you also may have found yourself slipping back to your usual side of the road or first language.

Listen to yourself

Old habits tend to crop up when we're tired, stressed or low on emotional resources. Don't admonish or judge yourself, take this as a 'message from yourself to yourself' that you need to recharge and replenish.

Keep up the good work

Like other practices, such as yoga, martial arts, music or language, you need to maintain some level of practice or you will get rusty. Practise the skills you found most useful. Do this when you *don't* immediately need them. You can practise better when not under duress, then you'll be prepared when you do need them. Below are suggestions for maintaining thought, emotion, and behaviour CBT skills.

Thought practice

Vivid pleasant moments

Practise your VPM from chapter 5 regularly, *even when you are not using it to stop an unpleasant thought.* Practise while you're waiting in queue, for example, or schedule regular practice – whichever way is easier for you to maintain a minimum of once a week practice. Why not further strengthen the brain circuits that underlie these lovely feelings? Who wouldn't want to 'live in' those circuits more often? Try these variations as well.

- Develop more VPMs from your memory – this can help you balance your understanding of your history, especially if it's been largely difficult.
- Collect new VPMs – use mindfulness to *not* miss the good parts of life.

Remember, these are *not* typically big, momentous occasions, but the brief interactions when we feel 'on line' with life, connected and fully present. As you become more mindful in your daily life and mood problems abate through CBT, you will notice more VPMs as they happen.

Emotion intelligence practice

Mindfulness is part of daily meditation for millions of people around the world. Why not join them. Mindfulness is another life skill that adds to our mental and physical wellbeing.

Breathing. Practise the breathing technique you preferred from chapter 7 (three-step or four-step breathing). This is a good skill to have in your 'tool kit' for life in general. Breathing techniques such as these are also part of meditation which has many physical and mental health benefits.

Ride the waves. Use the visual, sound or other method that worked best for you in chapter 7. To strengthen this skill, practise it when situations crop up that are *not* highly upsetting.

Behaviour Practice

Strengthen and expand

Are you saying things you wish you hadn't, before you know it? Are you *not* saying things and wished you had? Are you still agreeing to do too much? Don't worry, again, old habits die hard. Try these:

- You have the right to change your mind. You can tell the person you can't do what you agreed after all.
- It's not too late. If you find you wished you said things, but couldn't muster the nerve, if these are important, then make sure to communicate them.
- Rehearse difficult upcoming situations in your imagination.
- Practise a realistic version (not an idealised one).
- Rehearse how you might deal with likely problems.

The bigger picture

Feeling good doesn't happen just in your head. It happens in your head, which is attached to your body, which is involved in the world. The cornerstones to health, wellbeing and a satisfying life are: social connections; productivity; healthy eating; and regular exercise. (See the help list for resources on healthy diet and exercise.)

Social animals

Human beings are social animals, no less than bees. As infants, as mentioned in chapter 4, we will die without sufficient interaction human interaction, even if our physical needs are met. As adults, our immune systems, the bodily system that fights off infection and disease, changes within 20 minutes of our social situation. We secrete different sets of chemicals in our bodies and brains, depending on whether we've experienced defeat or triumph. People who have a broader range of friends across a variety of social circles have healthier immune systems. Whole fields of study examine these fascinating intersections between our social environment, our brains, bodies and psychologies, and CBT is one of the most useful of them.

Our mood states are very much affected by our social situations. Isolation and loneliness are huge problems and factors in our physical and mental health. Loneliness is a risk factor for heart and other diseases. With the ideal that we all have our own homes, cars and even televisions in every room, we can lead 'successful' lives but also discover that these lives increase isolation and loneliness.

We can't always control our access to people we like, nor our luck in meeting more, but we can learn important ways to increase our social connectedness, which is central to our health and wellbeing.

Social mindfulness

Research shows we do best with a social network including close relationships, as well as acquaintances. If you don't have a partner, but want one, it is easy to idealise what you will get from the relationship you hope for. What may seem like insignificant daily interactions are actually important. Really interact for that moment with the bus driver, the barista making your coffee, the person behind the till at the supermarket, the neighbours you recognise but don't know by name.

Social mindfulness methods

- Eye contact – be aware of it, even if fleeting – soak it up.
- Really look at people's faces when you're interacting with them.
- Stay present: Let thoughts about other things pass through your mind and let them go.
- What sort of feelings do you get when interacting with each individual?
- Imagine the scene occurring in slow motion.
- Pay attention to all your senses.

Increase your connections

Increase contact with the people you already enjoy and care about. Face-to-face is best, but phone calls, email and even social networking sites can all make a difference in how connected we feel. With the Internet, even international calling can be extraordinarily cheap (eg, Skype, or voice over IP address (VOIP) services).

Add something

Consider adding a regularly scheduled activity to your life. Check the Internet, local newspapers, libraries and community centres for activities and/or classes. You can also add a new habit such as reading the Sunday newspaper at a particular coffee shop or café. Adding a regular habit will give you the opportunity to be around another group of people; it takes time before you know if these will yield any friendship possibilities, but many free and inexpensive options exist out there. In general you want to:

- **Pick something you like** (*not* something that you think has the kind of people you should or would like to meet).
- **Don't say 'no' too quickly**. If you're trying something that meets regularly, go more than once before you decide if it's for you. Any one meeting can be less than optimal and the people you really get along with may not have come that time!
- **Try again.** Be realistic. You usually have to try a few pairs of shoes before you find the ones to buy – so don't be put off if the first thing(s) you try don't suit.

Productivity

Being useful and productive, especially in ways we enjoy, are critical to our happiness. Most of us feel better when we can see what we've accomplished. This does not have to be paid work. If you are not currently in education, working or volunteering, it is strongly recommended that you get involved in one of these activities. Check out organisations that can explain what your options are for education, work, and volunteering. Some of these are listed in the help section at the back of the book.

NB: Beware of 'accomplishment addiction'. Pursue activities because you enjoy them, *not* because you think they will reflect well on you. We are all subject to social pressures and concerns about what others think, but this can get out of balance. If you *only* pursue things because you need to collect more accomplishments, this will eventually fall flat and leave you empty and possibly depressed.

Life plans – balance is best

Have you ever thought about changing careers? Where you live? Who you live with? It is important to be honest with yourself about your life situation. There are no prizes for being unhappy in a job, partnership or living situation. But this also takes balanced consideration, as explained below.

If you're feeling very unwell, then it is not advisable to make large life changes in any sphere until you are feeling better. Yet, it is also important that you *do* consider if you have, or are heading towards, the life you want. This is not a dress rehearsal.

Avoiding the 'perfect life trap'

It is also important to try to figure out if you are overly attributing your unhappiness to things outside yourself. It is easy to think that changing these things will make us feel better. But this is a trap. Of course, it is possible to be in relationships, work or other situations that are not healthy and don't suit. But this is different than always thinking that your happiness depends on outside circumstances.

How many people do you know who break out of one relationship, only to find the next one with the same problems? Or leave one job because it's too stressful, only to find themselves in the next stressful job? The fact is the *only* thing you do have real control over is yourself, including your mind. And CBT is a set of methods for you to operate your mind to your best advantage.

It can be hard to tease apart what we truly want from the expectations we've absorbed from family, friends and society more generally. It can take a lot of courage to turn down an esteemed profession for one we feel is less esteemed, but enjoy more.

Chart 9B overleaf will help you plan your new activities/next steps. Under 'next steps', write anything you'd like to work on next, whether that's becoming more controlled in front of someone who winds you up, changing how much time you spend in a certain emotional state, redecorating your home, or looking for a new job – anything.

Chart 10B Next steps

Next step	First steps	Final goal

First steps include thinking about your next endeavour, looking into it (Internet, books, people who know about it). Your final goal may change over time as you learn more about it.

Lucid daydreaming

This exercise can help you think out of the box about your life and possibilities.

'Begin, the rest is easy.'

Fortune cookie.

- Pretend your life is a novel.
- 'You' are the main character in your novel.
- What does the protagonist do next?
- What adventures would this character not want to miss?
- What sort of life would they lead – job, location, partner, friends?

Take this exercise out and do it every so often, especially if you're feeling stuck in some aspect of your life.

Should I try a therapist?

It is possible to make the changes you want using books like this one and other resources. But, like any type of learning, having a teacher can help, in this case a therapist.

Different types of therapists

There are a bewildering number of mental health professionals, many of whom will have CBT training.

Below is a brief explanation of the different professions. The oversight bodies (and their websites) for each are in the help section. These websites list qualified professionals by geographical area.

Cognitive behavioural therapists

Specifically trained in CBT, come from a variety of clinical professions, including nursing, social work, counselling, psychology, and psychotherapy.

Counsellors

Talking therapists. An umbrella term for those trained in a variety of different talking therapies.

Psychiatrists

Medical doctors specialising in mental health who can prescribe medicine. It is very unlikely you would see a psychiatrist for talking therapy.

Psychologists

Talking therapists. There are a number of specialities in psychology. For therapy you are most likely to see a clinical or counselling psychologist.

Psychotherapists

Talking therapists with a focus on how our early development affects us.

National Health Service

CBT is increasingly available through the NHS. Contact your GP for a referral. Some areas have group CBT available, but not individual.

Private therapy

If you have private medical insurance, they will have lists of approved therapists.

If you don't have insurance, but are able to pay for private therapy, you can find qualified therapists in your area on the professional oversight bodies' websites in the help list. Many therapists have their own websites and you can find them by searching the Internet. It is best to stick with qualified therapists.

Finding one you like and get on with is key. Look at their websites, ask for a brochure about their practice and prices. If possible speak to them briefly to see if they sound like someone you could talk to.

Although you may not have a choice if you are going through the National Health Service, you may be able to request a male or a female if you have a preference.

Types of CBT

A growing number of types of therapy now include CBT methods. It's best to stick with evidence-based therapies. Accredited organisations, colleges, universities, governments, and health organisations are good sources of information if you want to know more about a type of therapy. Some evidence-based, specialised types of therapy that include CBT are listed below.

Cognitive analytic therapy (CAT)

Developed by Dr Anthony Ryle in North London, brings together analysis of your past and cultural-social factors that may be the basis of your current problems and then applies CBT (www.acat.me.uk).

Dialectical behavioral therapy (DBT)

Is a form of CBT developed by Dr Marsha Linehan to treat a serious mental health problem called 'borderline disorder', sometimes called borderline personality disorder. Other problems can also be successfully treated with DBT. Mindfulness and group therapy are part of DBT. (www.aculty.washington.edu/linehan/)

Schema therapy

Was developed by Dr Jeffrey Young and combines CBT with exploring the frameworks (schema) of the client's childhood and adult relationships. It was designed to treat long-entrenched maladaptive behavioral and emotional patterns, (also called personality disorders) (www.schematherapy.com).

Mindfulness-based cognitive therapy (MBCT)

This type of CBT was developed to help people who have repeated bouts of depression. Research shows that MBCT significantly reduces the chance of further depression and it has been endorsed by the UK National Institute of Clinical Excellence (NICE). It was developed by Drs Zindel Segal, Mark Williams and John Teasdale at Oxford University (www.mbct.co.uk) drawing from work by Jon Kabat-Zinn on mindfulness (see the help list).

Eclectic Approach

Many therapists will tell you they use an eclectic approach. This means they use methods from more than one type of therapy, drawing on different methods and theories as useful.

Summing Up

- CBT is a way of managing your mind. It increases health and wellbeing. It is best to incorporate CBT techniques as part of taking care of yourself, like other regular healthy habits. Don't wait for problems to arise. Choose some thought, emotion and behavioural CBT methods to keep up as a regular practice.
- A healthy mind can only be sustained with overall health including healthy eating and exercise, socialising sufficiently, and being useful and productive in our communities.
- The healthier we become, the more we will be able to consider life choices and options we may have always wanted to try, or hadn't thought we could manage before.
- If you choose to work with a therapist, you are best advised to find someone who is accredited in any one of the different types of therapies that include CBT in their treatment.

Glossary

Amygdala

The amygdala is a pair of almond-shaped brain structures located deep in the temporal lobes (the lobes on the sides of the brain). It is critical in early emotional development and bonding to our caregivers. It continues to play a crucial role in the formation of emotional memories, and controls fear responses, secretion of hormones, and general states of arousal.

Anxiety

Anxiety is a more mild form of fear. It includes feelings and thoughts of nervousness, worry, and trepidation. Anxiety is often accompanied by physical sensations including sweating, 'butterflies' in the stomach, the need to empty bowels and/or bladder, and need to leave the present situation – escape. Aches and pains in other parts of the body can also be caused by anxiety. Anxiety-related disorders are defined when these experiences interfere with, or significantly impact ordinary functioning. For specific diagnostic criteria, please refer to the ICD (International Classification of Disease) or the DSM (Diagnostic and Statistical Manual of Mental Disorders), both listed below.

Associative learning

Our tendency to believe there is a connection between things that happen together in time; a type of automatic learning that occurs when things co-occur.

Attachment

The term 'Attachment' now refers to the early, naturally occurring brain and psychological development generally starting after birth. It involves the complex interplay between the infant or child, and the relationship with caregivers. The dynamics, quality and content of our earliest relationships has a lasting impact on our psychology and brain organisation, in turn impacting all aspects of our behaviour including abilities to engage in cognitive activities such as school and work.

Avoidance learning
Avoidance learning occurs when we do 'x' in order to avoid 'y', for example, wearing a 'lucky' shirt to ensure a good interview. Such associations between doing 'x' to avoid 'y' tend to grow over time, unless purposefully stopped, often because we do not naturally test it – we don't not wear our 'lucky' shirt for an interview. Avoidance learning underlies many anxiety-related problems.

Cartesian dualism
In the mid-1600s René Descartes, the 'father of modern philosophy', successfully convinced the rulers in Europe that the mind and body are separate (Meditations on First Philosophy, 1641). Although a boon for the development of Western medicine, lifting the previous ban on surgeries and autopsies, this false belief that the mind and body are separate (often referred to as 'Cartesian dualism') has had terrible repercussions down the centuries, including fomenting stigma against mental health and its treatment.

Causality
When one thing makes another thing happen. We have a tendency to attribute causation, even when it is not really the case.

CBT
Cognitive behaviour therapy, or cognitive behavioural therapy, a type of talking therapy that focuses on changing how we think (cognition) and behave as a means of changing how we feel emotionally.

Co-dependence
Co-dependence is when you do too much for other people, in such a way as to be out of balance and unhealthy for both you and the other person. This tends to arise in those of us who had too many responsibilities as children. Left unchecked, co-dependence can spiral out of control and lead to depression. You can be co-dependent with other individuals, groups or even organisations such as where you work.

Depression
Feelings of sadness, lethargy, disinterest and more are all normal parts of life. When these experiences persist over time and interfere with ordinary functioning, you may have a depressive disorder. For specific diagnostic criteria, please refer to the ICD (International Classification of Disease) or the DSM (Diagnostic and Statistical Manual of Mental Disorders), both listed on the following page.

DSM-IV: Diagnostic and Statistical Manual of Mental Disorders – fourth edition
A diagnostic system for mental health problems used widely in North America, and increasingly used in other parts of the world. It is more detailed than the ICD. There are efforts to make these two systems the same for the next updated versions.

Embodied cognition
A branch of science that focuses on the ways our experiences in our minds are caused and influenced by our bodily functioning. This area of study postulates that all aspects of thinking, including maths, language and all others, are inextricably linked to our bodily functioning. This branch of science directly challenges the now defunct idea that the mind and body are separate (also called Cartesian dualism, see the previous page).

Emotional logic
Emotions follow their own set of natural laws that although different than those of geometry for example, can be helpful in understanding yourself and others. Some of these natural tendencies are described in studies of how people think such as the work of Kahneman and Teversky. (See *Thinking, Fast and Slow* in the book list.)

Hippocampus
The part of the brain that is involved in making and retrieving memories, spatial learning and more. It is found on both sides of the brain, deep within the temporal lobes (inward from your ears by about 4cm).

ICD – International Classification of Disease
The World Health Organisation's classification system for mental health and all health problems. www.who.int/classifications/icd/en/

Interoception
Our ability to sense our bodily functions and changes in them.

Learned helplessness
When faced with inescapable stress or pain, we can inevitably learn that nothing we do matters in the face of the stressor. This can make us inappropriately passive in the face of further challenges, and can cause depression. This was first discovered in animal studies done by Martin Seligman and his colleagues starting in the 1960s.

Lucid dreaming
The practice of purposefully managing your dreams as they occur. This is an ancient method that is still practised to good effect today, especially for reducing the bad effects of recurring nightmares. See the book and help lists for further information.

Meta-feelings
Emotional responses to our feelings. This term broadly includes thoughts and judgements we may also have about our feelings.

Mindfulness
Mindfulness refers to the practice of remaining very present in each current moment, experiencing life fully as it happens, rather than getting mired in thinking about the past or the future. Mindfulness has been practised since ancient times, and is core in some branches of Buddhism. It is also central in cognitive behaviour therapy (see the book and help lists).

Narrative style
Narrative style refers to our general style of speaking when saying more than just a few words. It's how we 'tell a story', although it can be what happened earlier in the day, for example, not a formal story. Research shows that whether we tell a meandering, organised, or truncated 'story' is related to the dynamics of our earliest relationships with parents or caregivers when we are children.

NATs
Negative automatic thoughts. Repeated, negative thoughts we have about ourselves, our pasts or our futures. We often don't notice them because we have them so often; they become part of our regular 'background' thinking. Stopping these has been shown to improve mood and wellbeing, and doing so is a cornerstone to CBT.

Neurons
Cells of the brain and spinal cord. They are static, don't move, and communicate using minute levels of electricity and chemicals which transfer across small gaps (synapses) between the neurons, as they do not touch. Neurons are made up of a cell body (soma), dendrites (fibres carrying incoming signals), and axons (longer fibres carrying outgoing signals).

NHS
National Health Service – the United Kingdom government organisation that provides health care to its inhabitants

NICE
National Institute for Health and Clinical Excellence – the United Kingdom government organisation that provides information on effective medical treatments, used as guidelines for the National Health Service (NHS).

Obsessive-compulsive disorder (OCD)
Obsessive-compulsive problems include the drive to do or think certain things repeatedly. Often it feels like doing these things keeps us or others safe. When these experiences interfere with ordinary functioning, you may meet the criteria for OCD. For specific diagnostic criteria, please refer to the ICD (International Classification of Disease) or the DSM (Diagnostic and Statistical Manual of Mental Disorders), both listed previously.

Panic attacks
Panic attacks are the result of the sudden onset of the full fear response, usually without being triggered by anything of significant real danger. Physical symptoms, including shortness of breath and a racing or irregular heartbeat, often serve to further increase the feelings of fear. People can think they are having a heart attack when they have their first panic attack. It is always sensible to seek medical intervention if you are not sure. For specific diagnostic criteria, please refer to the ICD (International Classification of Disease) or the DSM (Diagnostic and Statistical Manual of Mental Disorders), both listed previously.

Stress axis
The co-ordinated parts of the brain and body that orchestrate our reaction to stress. These include the pituitary and hypothalamus in the brain, and the adrenal glands (on top of the kidneys) that produce adrenalin. Normal reactions to stress include 'flight, fight or freeze'. It developed, in part, to help us respond to brief (and possibly life-threatening) events. In today's world, the stress axis is often engaged for long periods of time, and this is wearing on the body and brain tissues (see *Why Zebras Don't Get Ulcers: An Updated Guide to Stress* in the book list). In addition, the stress axis (also called the

hypothalamic-pituitary-adrenal axis, HPA) regulates other functions including emotions, sexual response, energy expenditure, digestion, and the immune system.

Superhero syndrome
Another name for co-dependence (see page 134).

Synapse
The small gap between neurons. Chemicals are released at the ends of the fibres extending from the neurons and are received by receptors on neighbouring neurons as means of communicating amongst these cells of the nervous system. This gap between neurons is also called the synaptic junction or synaptic cleft.

Vivid pleasant moments
Used in some of the core CBT techniques, vivid pleasant moments are generally taken from your past experiences and practised to have at the ready when you want to stop thinking negative and unproductive thoughts.

Help List

Academy of Cognitive Therapy

260 South Broad Street,18th Floor,Philadelphia, PA 19102, USA
Fax: +1 215 731 2182 (USA)
info@academyofct.org
www.academyofct.org
The US professional oversight body for cognitive therapists. Website has information about cognitive therapy (a type of CBT), links and lists of therapists accredited in the US.

Albert Ellis Institute

45 E. 65th Street, New York, NY 10065, USA
Tel: 1 212 535 0822 (USA)
info@albertellis.org
www.albertellisinstitute.org

Association for Cognitive Analytic Therapy (ACAT)

PO Box 6793, Dorchester, DT1 9DL
Tel: 0844 800 9496
admin@acat.me.uk
www.acat.me.uk
Information about cognitive analytic therapy. Lists CAT therapists.

Association for Rational Emotive Behaviour Therapy (AREBT)

c/o PO Box 177, Faversham, ME13 8WB
tracy@virtuallyorganised.com
www.arebt.org
Lists therapists accredited in rational emotive behaviour therapy.

Authentic Happiness

www.authentichappiness.sas.upenn.edu
The homepage of Dr. Martin Seligman, one of the founding CBT researchers. This site is about positive psychology, the psychology of increasing happiness and wellbeing.

Be Mindful Online – Managing Stress with Mindfulness.

Tel: 01273 325 136
www.bemindfulonline.com
Mental Health Foundation and Wellmind Media
Online course with audio downloads. Approximately £40. Free stress test online.

Beck Institute for Cognitive Behaviour Therapy (USA)

One Belmont Avenue, Suite 700, Bala Cynwyd, PA 19004-1610, USA
Tel: 1-610-664-3020
info@beckinstitute.org
www.beckinstitute.org
Training and resource centre for mental health and CBT information.

British Airways Flying with Confidence

01252 793 250 for booking courses and help if you are flying on British Airways
www.flyingwithconfidence.com
Courses for fear of flying offered in London and Edinburgh. Helpline open 24 hours a day.

British Association for Behavioural & Cognitive Psychotherapies (BABCP)

Imperial House, Hornby Street, Bury, Lancashire. BL9 5BN
Tel: 0161 705 4304
Fax: 0161 705 4306
babcp@babcp.com
www.babcp.com
The professional oversight organisation for CBT in the UK. List of therapists accredited with BABCP or with the Association for Rational Emotive Behaviour Therapy (AREBT).

British Association for Counselling & Psychotherapy (BACP)

Tel: 01455 883300
Text: 01455 550243
BACP House, 15 St John's Business Park, Lutterworth, Leicestershire LE17 4HB
bacp@bacp.co.uk
www.bacp.co.uk
Lists accredited therapists by location across the UK (including England, Scotland, Wales, Cornwall, and Northern Ireland).

British Psychological Society (BPS)

St Andrews House, 48 Princess Road East, Leicester, LE1 7DR
Tel: 0116 254 9568
Fax: 0116 227 1314
enquiries@bps.org.uk
www.bps.org.uk
Lists accredited psychologists by location across the UK (including England, Scotland, Wales, Cornwall, and Northern Ireland).

Bullying UK

Tel: 0808 800 2222 (Helpline: 7am – Midnight)
www.bullying.co.uk
Advice for parents, students and educators.

Counselling Directory IE

www.counsellingdirectory.ie
Ireland's largest independent directory of accredited counsellors/ psychotherapists and counselling/psychotherapy services. Over 1,200 listings.

Dialectical Behaviour Therapy Self Help (DBT Self Help)

www.dbtselfhelp.com
Online therapy help for people with borderline disorder or related symptoms.

Disability and the Equality Act 2010

www.direct.gov.uk/en/DisabledPeople/RightsAndObligations/DisabilityRights/DG_4001068

Information on the legal rights of those with disabilities, including having a mental health diagnosis, in relation to: employment; education; access to goods, services and facilities; transport; housing and more. This Act also provides rights for people not to be directly discriminated against or harassed because they have an association with a disabled person, including carers, partners, spouses or parents.

Family Lives

Parentline
Tel: 0808 800 2222 (Help Line: 7am – Midnight) Also provides advice for Bullying UK.
www.familylives.org.uk
Confidential support offered through online chat, email (through their website), text and the phone line above. Information on family relationships, teenagers, online safety, education, legal issues, health, and running a household.

International Association for the Study of Dreams

www.asdreams.org/index.htm
Non-profit organisation dedicated to research and information about dreaming, including about lucid dreaming.

Irish Council for Psychotherapy

73 Quinns Road, Shankill, Co. Dublin, Ireland.
Tel: 01-902 3819
www.psychotherapy-ireland.com
The professional oversight organisation for psychotherapists in Ireland. List of registered psychotherapists.

The Lucidity Institute

2155 Spencer St, Napa, California 94559, USA
Tel: 1 707 254 7829.
www.lucidity.com
Information and instruction on lucid dreaming, see the Lucid Dreaming FAQ page.

Mind

PO Box 277, Manchester, M60 3XN
Tel: 0300 123 3393 (Info line, Monday to Friday, 9am to 6pm)
info@mind.org.uk
Mind's Legal Advice Service
Tel: 0300 466 6463
legal@mind.org.uk
www.mind.org.uk
Website provides information about mental health problems, bullying at work, surviving abuse and addiction. Information for diagnosing problems is on the website. Legal information pertaining to those with mental health problems is provided. Lists local Mind advice and support groups.

Mind Cymru

3rd Floor, Quebec House, Castlebridge, Cowbridge Road East, Cardiff, CF11 9AB
Tel: 02920 39 51 23
contactwales@mind.org.uk
www.mind.org.uk/mind_cymru/landing
Website provides information about mental health problems, surviving abuse and addiction including diagnoses. Lists local Mind advice and support groups in Wales.

National Health Service

Scotland:
www.show.scot.nhs.uk

National Health Service Inform

www.nhsinform.co.uk
Provides basic health information and further links for more information.

National Institute for Health and Clinical Excellence (NICE)

London:
MidCity Place, 71 High Holborn, London, WC1V 6NA
Tel: 0845 003 7780
nice@nice.org.uk
Manchester:

Level 1A, City Tower, Piccadilly Plaza, Manchester, M1 4BD
Tel: 0845 003 7780
nice@nice.org.uk
www.nice.org.uk
An independent organisation providing national guidance on health-care delivery, treatment and other issues.

National Institute of Mental Health (NIMH)

6001 Executive Boulevard, Bethesda, Maryland 20892-9663, USA
1-301-443-4513 (USA)
1-866-615-6464 (toll-free in US)
1-301-443-4279 (US Fax)
nimhinfo@nih.gov
www.nimh.nih.gov
The world's largest and best-funded scientific research organisation focused on the understanding, treatment, and prevention of all mental illnesses and problems. Excellent resource for information on evidence-based treatments and the most up-to-date research on all mental health topics.

Oxford Mindfulness Centre

University of Oxford Department of Psychiatry,
Prince of Wales International Centre, Warneford Hospital, Oxford, OX3 7JX, UK
oxfordmindfulness.org
Information and resources about mindfulness. They run courses and workshops.

Psychological Society of Ireland

info@psihq.ie
www.psihq.ie
01 472 0105

Royal College of Psychiatrists

17 Belgrave Square, London SW1X 8PG
Tel: 020 7235 2351
Fax: 020 7245 1231
www.rcpsych.ac.uk

Excellent source for evidence-based information on all mental health problems and medication options for anxiety, bipolar disorder, depression, obsessive-compulsive disorder, panic, phobias, schizophrenia, and more.

Samaritans

Chris, PO Box 9090, Stirling, FK8 2SA
Tel: 08457 90 90 90 (Helpline UK)
1850 609090 (Helpline Republic of Ireland)
jo@samaritans.org
www.samaritans.org
24-hour telephone helpline offering confidential emotional support for people experiencing feelings of distress, upset or despair. In-person appointments are also available in some locations.

Sane

1st Floor Cityside House, 40 Adler Street, London, E1 1EE
Tel: 0845 767 8000 (helpline, 6pm – 11pm)
Tel: 020 7375 1002 Head office
info@sane.org.uk
sanemail@sane.org.uk (email support)
www.sane.org.uk
Provides information and support for people with mental health problems, family and friends.

Schema Therapy

Schema Therapy Institute, 130 West 42nd St., Ste. 501, New York, NY 10036 USA
Tel: 1-212-221-0700 (Monday-Friday, 9am until 4pm, US Eastern Time)
institute@schematherapy.com
www.schematherapy.com
Information, inventories about schemas, and resources for schema therapy (a type of CBT).

Scottish Association for Mental Health (SAMH)

Tel: 0141 530 1000
enquire@samh.org.uk
www.samh.org.uk/mental-health/where-to-get-help

Information service from Monday to Friday between, 2pm-4.30pm. Information service staff can answer general mental health enquiries, advise you on your rights and signpost you to your local services. They cannot provide medical advice, counselling, financial advice or representation, but they can direct you to other resources.

UK Council for Psychotherapy (UKCP)

2nd Floor, Edward House, 2 Wakley Street, London EC1V 7LT
Tel: 020 7014 9955
Fax: 020 7014 9977
info@ukcp.org.uk
www.psychotherapy.org.uk
Lists accredited psychotherapists (focus on attachment-related therapy) by location across the UK (including England, Scotland, Wales, and Northern Ireland).

Virgin Atlantic's Flying Without Fear Courses

01423 714900 Booking line
www.flyingwithoutfear.co.uk

Workplace Bullying, Stress, Employment Law, and You

www.workplacebullying.co.uk
Articles, the laws pertaining to bullying (legal resources), organisations and other resources.

Book List

Attachment Across the Lifecourse: A Brief Introduction
David Howe, Palgrave Macmillan, Basingstoke, Hampshire, UK, 2011. A good overview of attachment theory and research with moving examples of how the early attachment experience carries through the individuals' lives. Not a self-help book.

Behavior Therapy and Beyond (Master Work)
Arnold A. Lazarus, Jason Aronson Inc. Publishers of Rowman and Littlefield Publishing Group, Lanham, Maryland, USA, New edition, 1996. This is a newer edition of the 1971 classic of one of the early founders of cognitive behaviour therapy.

Brain Lock, Jeffrey M. Schwartz, HarperCollins
1st Regan Books/Harper Perennial Ed edition, London & New York, 1996

Depression: Causes and Treatment
Aaron T. Beck and Brad A. Alford, University of Pennsylvania Press, Philadelphia, USA, 2008. This is the new edition of Beck's classic text 40 years prior. Updated information, including on the biology of depression, has been added. An excellent read if you are interested in Beck's work from an academic point of view. This is not a self-help book.

Depressive Illness-Curse of the Strong
Tim Cantopher, Sheldon Press, London, 2003. Audio CD: Summersdale publishers, 2003.

Descartes' Error: Emotion, Reason and the Human Brain
Antonio Damasio, Putnam Publishing, New York, 1994; Random House, Vintage paperback, London, 2006. Fascinating case studies and explanations of the neuroscience of emotion and how it is indeed intertwined with rational thinking. Antonio Damasio together with his wife Hanna Damasio are one of the pre-eminent research teams in the neuroscience of emotion.

Embodied Cognition
Lawrence Shapiro, Routledge, London and New York, 2010. This is one of the first books available about this new field of how the brain tracks and utilises information from our bodies as part of our normal thinking process.

Emotions in Social Psychology: Essential Readings
(Key Readings in Social Psychology), W. Gerrod Parrott, Psychology Press, Philadelphia, Pennsylvania, USA, 2000.

Flourish: A New Understanding of Happiness and Well-Being – and How to Achieve Them
Martin E.P. Seligman, Nicholas Brealey Publishing, London and US, 2011. Martin Seligman discovered Learned Helplessness (as explained in chapter 8) and is one of the early developers of CBT methods. His most recent work focuses on how to increase happiness.

Guided Mindfulness Meditation [Audio CD]
Jon Kabat-Zinn, 2005

Happiness: A Guide to Developing Life's Most Important Skill
Matthieu Ricard, Little Brown and Company, New York, Boston and London, 2003 (English translation 2006)

Happiness: Lessons from a New Science (Second Edition)
Richard Layard, Penguin Books, London, 2005, 2011. Richard Layard is the Program Director for Wellbeing at the London School of Economics. This landmark book explains the science that shows us that wealth does not only not buy happiness, it appears to be inversely related. Depression, alcoholism and most human ills have increased dramatically in the industrialised nations over the last 50 years – a period of unprecedented increase in individual incomes. (NB: Professor Layard is also the director of a report to the UK government calling for 10,000 more CBT therapists, The Depression Report: A New Deal for Depression and Anxiety Disorders, 2006)

How to Stubbornly Refuse to Make Yourself Miserable About Anything – Yes, Anything!
Albert Ellis, Citadel Press, New York, 1988. This is an excellent, earthy, funny book drawing on 50 years' experience as a therapist by one of the most respected therapists of the last century. Excellent, direct advice and a delight to read.

Lucid Dreaming: A Concise Guide to Awakening in Your Dreams

Stephen LaBerge, Sounds True, Inc., Colorado, USA, 2009. Dr LaBerge, a professor in psychophysiology has done over 20 years of research in lucid dreaming. This is the paperback version of the original published in 1991 by Ballantine, with over 120,000 copies in print. These methods will help you strengthen your lucid dreaming ability, so you can then use the methods in chapter 9 to diffuse the power your past may continue to hold.

Mastery Of Obsessive-Compulsive Disorder: Client Kit
Edna B. Foa and Michael J. Kozak, Oxford University Press Oxford, England, 2004. (See *Stop Obsessing* on the next page.)

Meditations and Other Metaphysical Writings
Rene Descartes (Author), Desmond M. Clarke (Translator), Penguin Classics, London, 2003. This is the original philosophical writing that started the wrong notion of mind and body as separate, by 'the father of Western philosophy'. This new translation from the original Latin is more accessible. Additional philosophical writing of the period (mid-1600s) is included.

Mindfulness for Beginners [Audiobook; Audio CD]
Jon Kabat-Zinn, Sounds True Inc; Unabridged edition, Louisville, Colorado,80027, USA, 2006
Mindfulness is easier to learn through listening to instructions. Jon Kabat-Zinn is one of the leaders in mindfulness.

Overcoming Anxiety
Helen Kennerley, Constable & Robinson, London, 2009
CBT self-help book for anxiety.

Overcoming Traumatic Stress: A Self-help Guide Using Cognitive Behavioural Techniques
Claudia Herbert and Ann Wetmore, Robinson Publishing, London 2008. Clear, step-by-step methods for overcoming post-traumatic stress. Explanations of why you have the symptoms and experiences you do are included. Wetmore is therapist specialising in trauma recovery.

Pathological Altruism
Edited by Barbara Oakley, Ariel Knafo, Guruprasad Madhavan and David Sloan Wilson, Oxford University Press, Oxford, UK, 2011. This book brings together information from evolutionary biology, neuroscience, psychology and law, on the

topic of altruism -- doing for others selflessly. They describe research showing that over-developed altruism comes from unbalanced childhoods, and makes us more vulnerable to depression, work-related stress, and burnout among other problems.

Reinventing Your Life: The Breakthough Program to End Negative Behavior and Feel Great Again
Jeffrey E. Young and Janet S. Klosko, Plume of Penguin Publishing, New York and London, 1994. This book is based on Jeffrey Young's schema therapy and focuses on how to stop repeating the unwanted patterns learning in childhood.

Stop Obsessing: How To Overcome Your Obsessions And Compulsions
Edna B. Foa and Reid Wilson, Bantam Trade Paperback, New York, 2001. Excellent book by one of the world's preeminent researchers in treatment of OCD (Foa). This book is not for the feint-hearted, as she includes some earthy methods for overcoming obsessions and compulsions about germs and hygiene.

Talking Back to OCD: The Program That Helps Kids and Teens Say "No Way" -- and Parents Say "Way to Go"
John S March and Christine M Benton, The Guildford Press, New York, 2007. Although this book is aimed at young people, it is an excellent self-help book including detailed methods for everyone. John March is one of the top child psychiatrists worldwide.

Taming the Black Dog: How to Beat Depression – A Practical Manual for Sufferers, Their Relatives and Colleagues
Patrick Ellverton, How to Books, Oxford, UK, 2004.

The Boy Who Was Raised As a Dog: And Other Stories from a Child Psychiatrist's Notebook – What Traumatized Children Can Teach Us About Loss, Love, and Healing
Dr Bruce Perry and Maia Szalavitz, Basic Books, Perseus Books Group, 2008. Using moving real life examples, Perry and Szalavitz explain how early childhood experience impacts the developing brain and person, and how this impact carries forward. A good introduction to attachment science as discussed in Chapter 4.

The Committee of Sleep: How Artists, Scientists, and Athletes Use Dreams for Creative Problem-Solving—and How You Can Too
Deirdre Barrett. Crown (Random House), New York, 2001.

The Emotional Brain: The Mysterious Underpinnings of Emotional Life,
Joseph E. LeDoux, Simon & Schuster, New York, 1996, paperback edition Phoenix, Orion Books, Ltd, London, 1999. Joseph LeDoux is the discoverer of the short cut the brain uses for highly emotional information (see chapter 9).

The Grief Recovery Handbook: (20th Anniversary Edition): The Action Program for Moving Beyond Death, Divorce, and Other Losses
John W. James and Russell Friedman, Collins, London and New York , 2009

The Mindful Brain: Reflection and Attunement in the Cultivation of Well-Being
Daniel Siegel, W.W. Norton & Company, New York and London, 2007

The Molecules of Emotion: Why You Feel the Way You Feel
Candace Pert. Pocket Books, Simon & Schuster, New York, 1999. From the world-renowned scientist who first proved neurons have receptors for opiates (e.g. heroin) this book explores how chemicals interconnect our minds and bodies.

Thinking, Fast and Slow
Daniel Kahnman, Allen Lane, Penguin, New York, 2011. A world leader in the science of human decision-making, Kahneman reveals the often non-rational rules and impulses we all use regularly and how these natural tendencies affect our own happiness.

The Rough Guide to the Brain
Barry Gibb, Rough Guides, London, 2007. This is an excellent, succinct reference about brain function; clear, lively writing, with numerous helpful illustrations.

Wherever You Go, There You Are: Mindfulness Meditation In Everyday Life
Jon Kabat-Zinn, Hyperion, New York, 1994. Jon Kabat-Zinn is one of the world experts in mindfulness meditation.

Why Zebras Don't Get Ulcers: An Updated Guide to Stress, Stress Related Diseases, and Coping (2nd Edition)
Robert M. Sapolsky, Saint Martin's Press, Inc, New York, 2004. Excellent book about how stress affects the brain, mind and body by one of the pre-eminent researchers in the field.